A BATTLE
TOO FAR

With thanks to Henry for his wonderful descriptions, Lawrence for asking me to write this and Catherine Jones for proof reading.

A BATTLE TOO FAR

The True Story of
Rifleman Henry Taylor

By

Carole McEntee-Taylor

with

Rifleman Henry Taylor

Pen & Sword
MILITARY

First Published in Great Britain in 2013 by
PEN & SWORD MILITARY
an imprint of
Pen & Sword Books Ltd
47 Church Street, Barnsley, South Yorkshire S70 2AS

ISBN 978-1-78337-603-2

A CIP catalogue record for this book is
available from the British Library.

Typeset in 11/13.5pt Palatino by
Concept, Huddersfield

Printed and bound in England by
CPI Group (UK) Ltd, Croydon, CRO 4YY

Pen & Sword Books Ltd incorporates the imprints of Pen & Sword
Archaeology, Atlas, Aviation, Battleground, Discovery, Family History,
History, Maritime, Military, Naval, Politics, Railways, Select, Social History,
Transport, True Crime, Claymore Press, Frontline Books, Leo Cooper,
Praetorian Press, Remember When, Seaforth Publishing and Wharncliffe.

For a complete list of Pen & Sword titles please contact

PEN & SWORD BOOKS LIMITED
47 Church Street, Barnsley, South Yorkshire, S70 2AS, England
E-mail: enquiries@pen-and-sword.co.uk
Website: www.pen-and-sword.co.uk

Contents

As Henry wrote so much himself I have tried to allow him to tell the story without me drowning him out with too much background information. However, a certain amount is necessary to put it in context. I have tried to make the two voices blend.

Carole McEntee-Taylor

Foreword

Six battalions of The Rifle Brigade served overseas during the Second World War – the 1st, 2nd, 7th, 8th, 9th and 10th; the 7th and 8th originating from Territorial Army (TA) battalions of The London Rifle Brigade and the 9th and 10th from TA battalions of Tower Hamlets Rifles. Each has a proud war record and each has its own story to tell.

As Chairman of The Royal Green Jackets (Rifles) Museum in Winchester and custodian of the history and heritage of The Rifle Brigade, I always welcome new material entering the public domain which gives an account of the personal experiences of those who served in the Regiment's battalions. Invariably these accounts add something new and on occasions challenge directly the official record of events. They also add colour to otherwise dry Regimental and battalion histories. They tell us from the perspective of the individual about the trials and tribulations of service on the frontline, about the horrors of war, and often the lasting impact of the loss of close friends; about the humour – sometimes black humour – that prevailed as Riflemen sought relief from the sights, sounds and smell of battle and the fear that might otherwise have overcome them.

A Battle Too Far fits the bill admirably and is an invaluable addition to the Regimental archive. I anticipate its pages will be mined by military historians and researchers for years to come as they seek to bring to light snippets, indeed nuggets, of information which might otherwise remain unknown or forgotten. Above all, however, *A Battle Too Far* is more than the story of one man, Rifleman Henry Taylor. It is also testament to the actions, courage, commitment and sacrifice of all those who served in the 7th Battalion, The Rifle Brigade, during the Second World War.

Lt-Gen Sir Christopher Wallace
Winchester

Prologue

Port Said:
1 September 1945

As the ship pulled into Alex the dockside was a hive of activity. The captain had radioed ahead and so there was a battalion of the King's African Rifles (KAR) waiting to disarm us as we disembarked. All these KARs were standing at the order as a staff officer informed us that we were to be placed under arrest and escorted to Khartoum. Here we would contemplate our mutiny for two years. Our battalion was still under arms; the sound of the cocking of weapons greeted the officer's threat and a lone voice asked, 'And who's going to escort the darkies?' All our officers were powerless; we had the drop on the KARs, all that was needed was for someone to pull the trigger.

In the long, tense silence that followed Henry Taylor – 6923581, late 7th Battalion, The Rifle Brigade (1st Battalion London Rifle Brigade) – wondered how things could possibly have got this bad. Considering how fed up they were to be heading back to Egypt instead of going home to England, the evening had actually started quite well. There had certainly been no inkling of the trouble that was to come. Although his attention was focused totally on the situation now confronting him, Henry couldn't help casting his mind back over the momentous events of that evening: momentous events that could completely change his future, and not for the better.

It had all started on the lower deck of HMS *Strathmore* where they had been billeted with a ship full of New Zealanders on their way home after their three years' overseas service.

'Yep, not long now and we'll soon be home, back to our wives and sweethearts.' The tall, blonde New Zealander thrust his hips backwards and forwards a couple of times suggestively before continuing: 'Lots of good food, plenty of beer, and freedom from stupid rules and regulations. Can't wait eh?' He looked slowly round at his companions, paused for dramatic effect and then, smacking his hand loudly against his forehead, continued: 'Oh sorry lads I totally forgot, you're not going home are you?' His words were followed by lots of raucous laughter from the rest of his unit who were enjoying the opportunity to rub it in.

The men of the 7th Battalion Rifle Brigade had, for the most part, stoically ignored him. They'd had nothing but constant jibes and teasing from the 'Kiwis' since they had boarded the ship to head back to Egypt.

Henry or 'Horse' as he was known to the rest of his battalion, smiled wryly as he watched the deep blood-red sun sink rapidly into the deep blue of the Mediterranean Sea. The intense colour of the sun reminded him of the night they'd been travelling to the Mareth Line in Tunisia and he shivered suddenly. He hoped it wasn't an omen. He'd been away from home for over three years now, endured some of the heaviest fighting in North Africa, Italy and Austria, and still he wasn't being sent home.

He sighed inwardly; that was the army for you. When he'd enlisted the officer had asked him which corps he'd wanted to join. As a builder he'd asked for the Royal Engineers (RE) but they couldn't even get that right. The officer had misheard, either accidently or deliberately, and he'd ended up in the Rifle Brigade (RB) instead! Not that he'd have it any other way now although he would have liked to have gone home instead of another overseas posting to yet another potential war zone. The officer giving them their unwelcome orders had called it 'civil unrest' but to him and most of his friends, it was just another reason to stop him getting on with his life: a life that had been halted when he'd been conscripted in December 1941.

It wasn't only the fact that he couldn't go home that was depressing him. The battalion wasn't the same anymore. Many of his friends had gone back to England and their places taken by lots of younger conscripts. He sighed heavily as he deliberately pushed away thoughts of his friends, so many of whom wouldn't be coming back at all. At least he was alive and healthy even if he couldn't go home just yet. He wondered whether he would recognise England when he did finally get back. Three years was a long time to be away especially during a war. He frowned. It wasn't like him to be quite so morose. It must be because he was tired and fed up; tired of war, tired of killing, of having people try to kill him, tired of being permanently under orders, and definitely tired of travelling.

The sun had gone now, leaving in its place an inky-black sky filled with thousands upon thousands of bright twinkling stars; a poignant reminder of so many nights spent in various trenches and shell scrapes in the desert waiting for all hell to be let loose around him as they slowly and painfully pushed Rommel back to the sea.

His gloom deepened. Hadn't he done enough? He might not have been manning the guns at Snipe but being a stretcher bearer had put him in just as much danger, sometimes more, and having survived that he'd then endured the horrors of the bloody war in Tunisia. After that he'd almost got home, albeit en route to Normandy. But at the last minute, thanks to some trouble with the Greeks, he'd been sent to Italy instead where they'd fought their way up inch by inch against a determined defender with a definite advantage. But even that was not enough. As the war came to a close and he'd finally allowed himself to believe that he might soon be going home, they were given fresh orders to race to Klagenfurt in Austria and prevent it falling into the hands of Tito's partisans. Much as he and the rest of the battalion had liked Austria, he'd hoped against hope that this was the end of it; that finally he could go home to his family and a normal life where people weren't trying to kill him all the time. Some hope.

Instead the 7th Battalion the Rifle Brigade (7RB), together with the Black Watch, had been sent back to Egypt to put down civil unrest in Cairo. They'd endured a long but thankfully uneventful, train journey from Austria all the way back through Italy to Naples. And now here they were on a ship to Alexandria having to listen to a load of mouthy New Zealanders giving it the big one because they were lucky enough to be going home. The thought that he was probably just jealous crossed his mind and despite his depressed mood he smiled. No doubt in their place he would be doing exactly the same and enjoying every moment. No he couldn't really blame them. It wasn't their fault he was on his way back to Africa instead of going home.

Making a concerted effort to ignore the continuing jibes from the New Zealanders, he turned round and concentrated his attention on the other end of the lower deck where some music had just begun. The battalion now had its own band and to make the crossing easier they had elected to give a concert for the disgruntled men. For a while he listened as they played some of the more popular tunes of the day. Each one brought back memories of the last few years; some he wanted to remember, others he hoped he would eventually be able to forget. Lost in his thoughts he suddenly realised that the music had stopped and an argument was taking place. He stepped nearer and listened closely, his face darkening in anger as he realised that an officer from another regiment had decided to requisition the band for a dance on the upper deck with the service women who were on board. Ignoring the obvious anger his order had caused and the rapidly changing atmosphere, the officer arrogantly insisted the band follow him to the upper deck.

The men watched sullenly in silence as the band reluctantly began to pack up their instruments and headed after the officer. But it did not remain silent for long. What began as an angry murmuring gradually became louder and louder as the men began to vent their anger at what they saw as yet another example of the unfairness with which they had been treated.

He could never really remember what happened next, whether someone had suggested they follow or whether it had just happened. But suddenly he found himself locked into a throng of angry, resentful men heading purposefully for the upper deck. Reaching it they found their way barred by men from the other regiment. After exchanging insults for a few moments they began to turn back, when suddenly everything changed. It seemed to him that everything happened at once. Shouts rang out, men began pushing forward and within seconds they had shoved their way through the men barring their way and stormed the upper deck, scattering all and sundry to the cheers and encouragement of the watching New Zealanders:

> Our officers did not interfere but stood to one side sipping their whiskey and sodas while taking note of the ring leaders. The ship's RSM tried to restore order by standing on a chair and attempting to read the riot act; he was sent flying and broke his leg. Another ship's officer was threatened with being thrown over the side, and some of the blokes stormed the engine room and stopped the ship. We now had a mutiny on our hands.

While some of the men had taken control of the engine room, others had stormed the bridge. They now had total control over the ship and it started to go round and round in circles. The stalemate continued for some time with the ship going round in circles and the men still rioting. The officers had no intention of getting between the determined, very experienced Riflemen and their objective of getting their band back. They remained quietly aloof, watching and waiting for an opportunity to calm things down:

> Finally they did and we made a request to our officers for our band back. Then we would return the ship to the control of the crew. Eventually the band was returned and we continued our passage to Alexandria.

The band had now returned to the lower deck and things began to quieten down. Thinking they had won and feeling justified at their action, the men settled down happily to enjoy the music. However, this would not be the end of it. As the ship sailed on, plans were rapidly put in place for when they arrived in Alexandria.

Chapter 1

23 October 1942:
Up the Blue

The Very light hovered gracefully above them and illuminated the night sky for what seemed like an interminable age before beginning its rapid descent back to earth. The evening was cold and it had just started to drizzle; a continuous stream of rain that stung their sunburnt faces as they waited impatiently for the order to advance. Henry glanced quickly at the other men around him. Like him their faces had turned skyward when the Very light had shot up. But before he could speak, the air was filled with ear-splitting noise and the brilliant flashes of the massive heavy artillery bombardment as shelling began on the German positions. They had no time to adjust to the noise as it was swiftly followed by the heavy shells of the Royal Navy ships pounding the German defences. The strange whining sound of the heavy shells as they shrieked across the sky took Henry by surprise. It was not what he had expected but he had no time to think about it as high above, in the brief gaps between shelling, he could just about make out the RAF Desert Air force utilising their superior air power and bombing German positions. To Henry, other than the presence of the RAF, it was reminiscent of the films he'd seen about the Great War. But this was no film, this was real. Operation Lightfoot, the beginning of the second battle of El-Alamein, had begun and Henry had a ringside seat.

Italy had entered the Second World War in June 1940. The Italian colony of Libya bordered the vital British protectorate of Egypt and

1

the war then quickly spread to North Africa. Marshall Graziani's troops began their land offensive on 7 September 1940 and initially their superiority in numbers gave them success. After capturing the port of Sidi el-Barrini, they began to establish a chain of fortified camps. In December 1940 the British, led by Generals Wavell and O'Connor, counter-attacked and quickly defeated the Italians. As Italian supplies dwindled British armaments grew, and this eventually led to the Italian forces retreating in chaos. However, so many soldiers surrendered that they slowed the movement of the British tanks which impeded the Allied advance. Meanwhile, shocked by the Italian failure, Hitler dispatched General Erwin Rommel and the German Afrika Corps to prevent the total collapse of Italian forces.

The 'Desert Fox', as Rommel became known, soon adapted his tactics to suit the conditions. The desert had vast open areas with few obstacles and a relatively small civilian population. This allowed him to sweep round the enemy at speed from behind and outflank them. His first attack on the Sollum-Halfaya line on the Egyptian border in February 1941 caught the British by surprise and he soon took Benghazi before moving on to besiege Tobruk.

The British attempted to liberate Tobruk in June 1941 through Operation Battleaxe, but were defeated by Rommel's well-prepared defences. General Wavell was replaced by General Auchinleck and in November Operation Crusader was launched, which this time caught Rommel by surprise. Despite the havoc wreaked by their 88mm guns, the Germans took heavy losses and with dwindling supplies were forced to retreat back to El Agheila, which was where they had started from in March. The British finally succeeded in liberating Tobruk and Benghazi at the end of 1941.

The provision of supplies played a crucial part of the war in North Africa. While the British received material from depots in nearby Alexandria, the Axis supplies had to come from Tripoli. Their position was further compounded because Britain still held the island of Malta. This allowed the British to attack Axis convoys crossing the Mediterranean. But despite these advantages, British supply lines had become over extended by the beginning of 1942. This gave Rommel the opportunity to counter-attack, forcing the British to retreat to the defensive positions known as the Gazala Line.

The Battle of Gazala was one of the fiercest of the Desert War and resulted in the retreat of Auchinleck's men back to Alam Halfa. Tobruk was cut off once again and fell rapidly back into the hands of the Axis forces.

But gradually things began to change. By August 1942 only a third of the supplies Rommel needed were getting through to him. In contrast the Allies were able to bring in vast supplies as they controlled the Suez Canal and were still dominating the Mediterranean. Aware that his situation was likely to deteriorate, Rommel decided to attack even though he lacked the necessary equipment. The Allies knew that if the Afrika Corps was to reach Suez their own capacity to re-supply would be severely curtailed as the alternative supply route would have to be via South Africa. This was a long and considerably more dangerous route, not least because of the vagaries of the weather. It was also important that the Germans did not defeat the Allies in North Africa as not only would this be a severe psychological blow but would also give Germany virtually free access to the oil in the Middle East. Thus El Alamein was effectively a last stand for the Allies in North Africa.

To the north of El Alamein was the Mediterranean Sea and to the south was the Qattara Depression. El Alamein was a bottleneck that would effectively prevent Rommel from using his favoured form of attack – sweeping onto the enemy from the rear. Rommel therefore decided to attack in the south. Lieutenant General B.L. Montgomery, who now commanded 8th Army, knew this because the code breakers at Bletchley Park had a copy of Rommel's battle plan and had deciphered the code. Montgomery not only knew the battle plan and the supply routes, he also knew that Rommel was very short of petrol and therefore could not sustain a long campaign. It is said that so confident was Montgomery of success that when Rommel attacked and he was woken from his sleep to be given the news, he said 'Excellent, excellent' and promptly went back to sleep.

As Rommel's Panzers attacked they were severely hit by the large number of land mines laid by the Allies at Alam Halfa and those that weren't destroyed were held up and became easy pickings for Allied fighter planes. Things looked bleak for Rommel but as he ordered his tanks north a sandstorm blew up and this provided his tanks with cover from the Allied planes. Once the sandstorm had cleared, his tanks came under renewed fire from Allied bombers and he was finally left with no choice but to retreat, fully expecting the 8th Army to follow.

But Monty was in no hurry. He was waiting for the arrival of his 'swallows', 300 Sherman tanks, equipped with 75mm guns which could penetrate a Panzer's armour at over a 1,000 metres. So, instead of pursuing the retreating Axis forces, he ordered his men to dig in and form a defensive line. In the meantime he planned the next phase of the attack.

Rommel was dug in deep in defensive positions protected by minefields. Known as the 'Devil's Garden' these were up to five miles deep in some places and were littered with anti-tank and anti-personnel mines. The biggest problem for Monty would be getting through these minefields. To give himself as much chance as possible he launched Operation Bertram. This was designed to convince Rommel that the full weight of the 8th Army would be concentrated in the south. Dummy tanks were erected in the region and a dummy pipeline was slowly constructed in an attempt to convince Rommel that the Allies were in no hurry to attack. In the north tanks were covered so that from the air they appeared to be lorries. The deception worked well and Rommel became convinced that the main thrust of the attack would be in the south.

Because Rommel lacked fuel and sufficient numbers to match the Allies in an open tank battle he had to try and restrict it to the areas he already defended and counter any breakthrough quickly. He stiffened his defensive lines by alternating German and Italian infantry. But because Operation Bertram had succeeded in confusing him as to where the actual attack would be he split his armoured forces into a northern group (15th Panzer and Littorio Divisions) and a southern group (21st Panzer and Ariete Divisions). His intention was to be able to counter any armoured attack as quickly as possible so that no breakthrough was achieved. Although this meant he had a significant proportion of his armour nearer the front of his lines he still had the 90th Light and Trieste motorised divisions in reserve which he believed he could manoeuvre quicker than the Allies could advance. However, when he did come to mobilise them, he was unable to do so because of a chronic lack of fuel.

With the arrival of the two fresh infantry divisions and another two armoured divisions from England, the British now had eighty infantry battalions to Rommel's seventy and, apart from anti-tank devices, also had more equipment. The British had 480 medium tanks of which 270 were Shermans, 600 medium and light tanks, eighty-five infantry battalions, 856 field artillery, sixty medium artillery and 850 six-pounders or their equivalent, although some battalions still only had 2-pounders.

In contrast, the Germans only had 218 tanks of which thirty were Mk IV Specials, thirty-one medium tanks, thirty-one infantry battalions, 200 field artillery, twenty-nine heavy field artillery, 154 ack-ack guns and 300 six-pounders or their equivalent. Their Italian allies were even more poorly equipped with only 278 poor-quality tanks, forty-one infantry battalions and 350 ill-organized and limited range field artillery. Furthermore, unlike the British, Rommel was also short of petrol.

The British also had six-pounder anti-tank guns which had reduced Rommel's tanks to light protective duties only. This meant he was unlikely to use the tanks in a counter-attack if the British were ready for him. Instead, he would use his infantry and anti-tank blocking force wherever he thought the British could penetrate.

The Allies reasoned that the gap between the forces was not big enough to risk too much offensive scrapping. Therefore the tactic was to start the battle as an artillery battle and end with it being armoured. For this they needed to break through and out manoeuvre the anti-tank screens. The British knew that Rommel had to hold the main coastal road behind him so his intention would be to hold the north even if he conceded territory to the south.

The diversionary attack in the south was intended to occupy up to fifty per cent of Rommel's forces, whilst the real attack in the north was intended to take just one night. It was called Operation Lightfoot for the simple reason that the infantry would attack first through the minefields as they were not heavy enough to trigger the anti-tank mines. As the infantry attacked so the engineers would clear a 24ft-wide path for the tanks. Their task was extremely dangerous

5

as the mines were often inter connected with other mines via wires, so setting off one could set off a chain of explosions.

XXX Corps consisted of 1st Armoured Division and 10th Armoured Division. The latter consisted of the 8th Armoured Brigade, 133rd Lorried Infantry Brigade and 24th Armoured Brigade. The 1st Armoured Division consisted of 2nd Armoured Brigade and 7th Motor Brigade.

The 7th Motor Brigade consisted of 2RB (Rifle Brigade), 7RB (Rifle Brigade) and 2KRRC (Kings Royal Rifle Corps) brigaded together and recently transferred from the 7th Armoured Division. The task for both armoured divisions was to pass through the gaps in the minefields, 10th Armoured Division to the south and 1st Armoured Division to the north. The plan was that once through the minefields the armour would continue through the infantry, which would have already reached its objective line and advance about a mile to their own objective codenamed 'Pierson'.

Henry was a member of 7th Motor Brigade so he was positioned in the north where the thrust of the main attack was. As the barrage continued, he closed his eyes momentarily to say a quick prayer. It wouldn't be long now and it would be time to move forward.

By now the Germans were returning fire and the counter barrage was crashing down into the Allied artillery. The noise was deafening and his eardrums felt as if they would burst. Even from his lowly vantage position Henry could see that the advantage was with the Allies. The ratio of shelling was at least ten to one and sometimes as much as twenty to one. The front they were due to attack was twenty-five miles long from escarpment to sea and a 25lb gun had been placed every twenty-five yards. Behind them were 60lb guns and behind them the Howitzers. At the rear was the Royal Navy with its 16-inch and 20-inch guns. His ears were now hurting from the constant noise and his throat began to burn as the air was filled with smoke, dust, sand and the acrid smell of cordite. Visibility was virtually zero and he began to wonder how on earth they would find their positions.

There were three gaps through the German minefields: Sun, Moon and Star. They had spent all day punching star, moon or sun-shaped holes in old petrol cans which would then hold hurricane lamps. These would hang from posts driven into the ground along the edge of each of the gaps that had been cleared by the engineers. It was these lamps that would guide the tanks safely through the minefields.

By 8pm that evening they had all moved into position with the Bren gun carriers at the front, the Rifle platoons behind them and the gunners to the rear. Once in position they waited impatiently for the barrage to start. This was due at 10pm and once the bombardment had finished the plan was for the tanks to move through the gaps cleared by the engineers in the German minefields.

The Bren gun carriers had the job of protecting the engineers as they defused the mines. Behind them came the platoons banging iron stakes into the ground and hanging up the tins with the lamps inside. These were placed facing backwards towards the British lines to guide the advance:

> My duties were to stand with one of these lamps while our tanks passed by. Opposite was another rifleman by the name of George Spencer. Known to everyone later by his nickname 'Spanner', George was to marry my eldest sister and become my brother-in-law.

Behind them came the main infantry units who would clear out the German frontlines and behind them came the tanks. But first they had to wait for the bombardment to cease. Henry knew from the little information the more experienced riflemen had given that this was always the worst time: the waiting to advance. But for him and the other raw recruits there was the additional worry of how they would react when the real fighting started. For Henry and many others, the fear of disgracing himself far outweighed the fear of the actual fighting. In an effort to distract himself he cast his mind back over how much his life had changed over the past few months:

> I was conscripted into the British Army in 1941. My medical board examination took place at Edgeware, Middlesex, in December where I was confronted by a venerable gentleman in army uniform who seemed to have more pips on

his shoulders than an orange. This shrewd old gent looked me up and down, asked a few questions, and then wrote down his conclusions before passing me on to a medical officer. After the usual formalities, I returned to the officer with all the pips who asked what corps of the army I wished to join. As a builder I replied, 'the RE's'. He must have misheard or had already decided, for he wrote down RBs. From then on I was on the road to Armageddon.

I knew nothing about the Rifle Brigade until I reached Winchester a few days before Christmas 1941. As I left home in Enfield my dad's cousin had warned me that I was in for a busy time, as he had served with the King's Royal Rifle Corp in the trenches of the Great War. My draft arrived at Winchester Railway Station before first light on 18 December 1941. We were met by the regimental band and a Company Sergeant Major, fallen into ranks and then, as the sun rose, marched through Winchester. As we neared the Peninsular Barracks, the band struck up 'I'm 95', the regimental march. It must have been impressive as they turned out the guard as we entered the barracks.

We cooled our heels in Winchester over the Christmas. Why call us up at this time when everyone else had gone on leave? Our training, when it started, lasted three months. We were under the care of three NCOs, a sergeant, a corporal and a lance corporal and these men instructed us on the finer arts of soldiering with the Rifle Brigade. At the end of the three months we were proficient in thirteen weapons and able to drive. Now came the schemes on Salisbury Plain to hone our fighting techniques. We travelled to Tidworth Camp and spent the next weeks mainly getting lost among the wilds of Wiltshire.

When our stint at Tidworth was completed our draft were granted forty-eight hours embarkation leave. We left England in April 1942. I had just turned twenty and did not return home for the next three-and-a-half years. Our ship, the *Empress of Japan* left Liverpool en route for Egypt. The convoy took eight weeks to travel around the Cape, past

Aden, and then docked at Port Said. Embarkation of the troops proceeded using rafts and it must have looked like a scene from the film *The Four Feathers*. Although we were replacements for the Rifle Brigade Battalions already in the desert, we had not yet been assigned to anyone in particular.

The rest of our journey to 8th Army's concentration area took place by train to El-Geneifa where we began our desert acclimatization and started to get used to our daily water ration.

The camp at El-Geneifa spread out over fifteen miles and consisted mostly of tents, some of which were out of sight of the main complex. The ground was completely flat and the wind howled across it consistently, covering everything and anything in a fine dusting of sand. It was later used as a POW camp for German POWs.

The water ration amounted to one-and-a-half pints, which was supposed to be used for all of our ablutions, and what was left was for drinking and for making tea. Water is a scarce commodity in the desert; it dictates the tactics and the size of the army. To counter this, 8th Army laid a pipe line to convey water to large prefabricated reservoirs made of rubber, and organized water runs using Royal Navy Destroyers along the coast. As we acclimatized the route marches began, usually fifteen miles, and some even around the great pyramids at Giza. After a fortnight of these marches, we again boarded a train and set off 'up the blue' towards Alamein.

'The Blue' was the name the soldiers had given to the harsh unforgiving desert where they were fighting. Inland from the coast there were no birds and virtually no vegetation other than camel thorn, instead there were flies, fleas, sickness and considerable danger from enemy artillery, dive bombers, Panzer and infantry assaults. The desert over which they fought was not an endless expanse of golden sand but rather a dirty brownish gritty crust, a result of

9

erosion of the limestone rock over the centuries. Behind the narrow strip of fertile and intensely-cultivated plain were sheer limestone cliffs (djebel) which in some places rose vertically out of the sea. The crumbling surfaces and steep inclines made these cliffs virtually impassable to anything other than tracked vehicles.

The limestone plateau that extended gently southwards from the cliffs was littered with stones, rocks and a layer of grit which in some places was several feet deep. Low ridges and hills had formed from harder rock which had not eroded and it was these that were fiercely fought over as they provided natural observation points.

In other areas the limestone was softer and erosion had formed depressions (deir) which in turn provided natural defensive positions and obstacles. The biggest of these was called the Qattara which was thousands of square miles across, had sheer, impassable cliffs and was several hundred feet deep.

Further south there were rolling sand dunes which hampered mobility for anything other than the Long Range Desert Group and SAS who were based there. This effectively penned the armies in a narrow strip of land, over 1,000 miles long but less than seventy miles wide between the Mediterranean to the north and the impenetrable sand dunes of the south.

There was only one main road that was passable in all weathers and any other movement used the native tracks known as 'trigh'. These were often quite wide but progress was slow as the heavy vehicles damaged the surface creating deep ruts. To avoid these ruts which would break vehicle springs, the drivers used the edges of the trigh making them even wider. The sand that lined the trigh was fine, powdery and a reddish yellow. It frequently clogged air filters and threw up considerable clouds of dust which penetrated clothing, weapons and vehicles as well as the soldiers' eyes and mouths. In the winter the heavy rains turned the sand into mud which completely immobilised the vehicles.

The XXX Corps formation area extended from the British mine-fields to its rear headquarters at El Hamman. On an east-west line spread out along the Corps' borderline were defence boxes that had been originally constructed to defend against any attacks from the Axis (German and Italian) forces. Now these were no longer needed they were being used as bases with concentrations of tanks, armoured vehicles, shells, stores and men. All were waiting for Operation Lightfoot to begin. The majority of the rear troops were camped along the coast with others in various set areas and awaiting their orders to advance. It was to this enormous camp that Henry and his fellow Riflemen finally arrived:

> Our rations when we arrived consisted of cold meat and vegetable stew (M&V) served up from a tin bath using a ladle by two riflemen.

A particularly loud bang bought his attention sharply back to the present. Far from diminishing, the bombardment appeared to be getting worse. The noise was totally deafening, the ground was shaking and even in the dark he could see sand, dust and debris flying high into the sky as the shells hit their targets. If he looked in the direction of the sea he could just make out the flashes of the naval guns from the warships. Henry began to wonder whether anyone could possibly have survived such a devastating barrage. Then, twenty minutes after its abrupt start, it finished. The sudden silence caught him by surprise and then they were given the order to advance.

Henry could just hear the cheers from the whole company echoing round him and see glimpses of the engineers who were lying on their stomachs and prodding gently but urgently for mines with their bayonets. Then they began to move slowly forward. It seemed hardly any time at all before he was allocated a spot and he began hurriedly banging in his metal rod. Within seconds it was firmly embedded and he hung his lamp after first having lit it. As his fellow Riflemen did the same, the area began to look more like Oxford Street than a battlefield as lights appeared everywhere and then the mortars opened up.

The air was now filled with different sounds with machine guns rattling noisily. Mortars were whooshing through the air as they rained down on the advancing troops. There was the single tap, tap, tap from individual rifles and shouts and yells which echoed off into the distance. Henry began to feel useless. He also became increasingly

11

aware that standing beside a lighted lantern in the middle of a battlefield made him a perfect target. Trying not to think too much about it he concentrated his attention on the activity going on around him. He watched transfixed as a lone piper, lit up in the sporadic fire, walked erect in the distance and headed slowly forward followed by the Scots with their fixed bayonets. The lonely sound of the lament in the distance merged with the cries of the wounded and dying and still the horrendous noise of the battle continued raging all around him. Yet he could do nothing: he couldn't leave his place, by his lamp, guiding in the tanks. He was part of it but not part of it and, despite the horror all around him, he longed to be in the thick of it with his mates.

It was now past midnight and the night was bitterly cold. Slowly the tanks trundled past, their heavy engines unheard in the furious counter barrage that was pounding the Allied advance. Fiery, glowing-red balls slammed against the armoured plates of the Shermans while shrieking, whistling 88mm shot hurtled towards the unprotected infantry. The narrow stretch of cleared land proved to be the downfall of the operation as it only took one non-moving tank to block the way, leaving the rest to be easy targets for the feared German 88mm dual-purpose gun. Although the leading squadrons continued their slow advance at the regulation pace of 3mph, they finally ground to a halt as they came across increased resistance and stalled infantry units frantically digging in.

As the sun rose the full horror of the battle became apparent. The ground was littered with 'brewed up' tanks and the burnt and unrecognisable bodies of the crews intermingled with the lifeless mangled corpses of the infantry. As Henry took in the hellish scene before him he looked across at George and was relieved to see he too was alive and uninjured and realised just how lucky he had been to survive.

Chapter 2

26 October 1942:
A Dead Dodgy Job

The main battle was now concentrated around Tel el Aqqaqir and a series of ridges called Kidney, Woodcock and Snipe. Woodcock lay roughly a mile north-west of Kidney with Snipe roughly the same distance to the south-west:

> The motor battalions of the Rifle Brigade and the King's Royal Rifle Corp had been grouped together to form 7th Motor Brigade. Their task was to spearhead the British Armoured advance by taking a series of ridges known to 8th Army as Kidney, Snipe and Woodcock. Here they were to dig in and hold at all costs.

The plan was that on 26 October at 23.00 the 2nd Battalion the Rifle Brigade would attack Snipe and the 2nd Battalion the King's Royal Rifle Corps (KRRC) would attack Woodcock. The following dawn would see the 2nd Armoured Brigade pass to the north of Woodcock while the 24th Armoured Brigade would pass to the south of Snipe supported by all the artillery from both XXX and X Corps. At least that was the plan. In the dark both battalions had trouble finding their objectives and they were further hampered by the clouds of dust that were thrown up by the movement of their vehicles. By dawn the KRRC had to find cover and dig in some distance from Woodcock. The Rifle Brigade initially encountered little opposition and, having found what they thought was their position, dug in.

At 06.00 on 27 October the 2nd Armoured Brigade began their advance but encountered such heavy opposition that by noon they still hadn't been able to link with the KRRC. The 24th Armoured brigade started later but did make contact with the Rifle Brigade after initially shelling them in error. For the next few hours they fought continuously against battle groups from the Italian Littorio mechanized division and 15th Panzer Division. The Rifle Brigade endured constant mortar and shelling all day then at 16.00 Rommel launched a major counter-attack with the 90th Light and 21st Panzer Divisions.

All the Rifle Brigade had to defend themselves with were thirteen six-pounder anti-tank guns plus six more from the 239th Anti-tank Battery (RA), grouped around an old Italian position. At risk of being overrun several times they nevertheless held their ground, in the process destroying twenty-two German and ten Italian tanks:

> The motor battalion's actions at these ridges passed into legend within 8th Army, and the 2nd battalion of the Rifle Brigade won the regiment's only Victoria Cross of the war at Snipe.

Eventually the Germans gave up and withdrew but no one realised this so the Rifle Brigade were withdrawn without being replaced and this allowed the Germans to move back in unopposed.

Henry was delighted to hear that the Rifle Brigade would be in line for a Victoria Cross but disgusted that despite the heavy fighting raging all around him he had still not been assigned a fighting role:

> While these battles raged, I had been found another job behind the 7th Battalion, Rifle Brigade's position opposite the Rahman track. From standing around holding a lantern I now found myself as a battalion stretcher bearer. My training consisted of a quick visit to the Regimental Aid Post to pick up a Red Cross armband, meet the other three riflemen who made up our crew, and be issued a stretcher.

However, it wasn't long before his first impression that yet again he'd been given a rather cushy job vanished as he realized that in some ways being a stretcher bearer was actually much worse than being in the heat of battle where at least he would have been able to defend himself:

> Casualties began coming back from the battles raging around Kidney and the other ridges. British Armour had been involved and wounded Tanki Wallahs stumbled back, many badly burnt, along with infantrymen. Being a stretcher bearer is a dead dodgy job with very little opportunity to take cover and you are exposed to fire nearly all the time. I remember the dead piled up like logs outside the aid posts. Some had been there for a couple of days and the pile moved with thousands upon thousands of maggots.
>
> German resistance to Lightfoot began to stiffen and casualties began to mount, so 8th Army, while still keeping up the pressure, paused and prepared for a second attempt to break through the German defences. This second operation was codenamed Supercharge and 8th Army was to smash its way through the German defences irrespective of losses and release British Armour into the open desert.

It was not just the Allies who had taken heavy casualties during Operation Lightfoot. Rommel had only 300 tanks left in contrast to the Allies who still had over 900. The Australians now attacked by the Mediterranean and Rommel withdrew his tanks to send them north. Convinced that Monty was going to attack here, Rommel also moved a large part of the Afrika Corps north, giving Monty room to manoeuvre. The Australians took many casualties but it was their attack that changed the course of the battle.

Monty now launched Operation Supercharge, a British and New Zealand infantry attack south of where the Australians were fighting and caught Rommel by surprise.

Operation Supercharge should have started on 31 October but there wasn't time to organize it properly so it was delayed until 2 November at 01.00. The task of the two British Brigades was to push a 4,000-yard-wide salient into enemy lines to the depth of 4,000 yards. This objective was about 800 yards east of the Rahman

Track and a little to the north of Tel el Aqaqir, the highest point on the low ridge of Aqaqir. As the flanks were the weakest part of the spearhead, it was expected that the enemy would pour a continuous barrage of fire onto the advancing brigades so additional infantry would be used. On the left or southern flank, 133 Brigade, three battalions of The Sussex Regiment, would storm Woodcock while on the northern flank the 28th (Maori) Battalion of the New Zealand Division would attack the area around point 29.

The infantry battalions were withdrawn from the frontline trenches just before the artillery bombardment began at 01.05, which in turn was ten minutes after the two brigades had crossed their start line. The intention was for the bombardment to continue to fall on the abandoned frontline until the infantry reached it. Then some of the artillery would begin targeting known enemy gun positions while the rest would continue to lay a steady barrage across the ground on which they were advancing. Prior to this there had been seven hours of air raids on both the Rahman track and Aqaqir Ridge.

The ground they were to advance across was expected to be littered with small areas of indiscriminately-sown explosive devices. Set among these there would be well-sited infantry positions equipped with machine guns, mortars and tank turrets dug into the hard rock surface. Behind these positions were successive lines of gun pits. These would provide crossfire directed by command posts that had been dug deep underground. Anti-tank lines had been extended to a great depth both in front of and beyond the Rahman track but as these were quite recent their exact location was unknown and they were so well dug in that they were virtually undetectable from ground level except at close range.

It was accepted wisdom that for tanks to successfully attack gun lines, the ratio of tanks to guns should be considerably in favour of the tanks. But Monty lacked sufficient infantry so had been left with little option but to use armour to charge the guns even though he knew that the tanks would sustain considerable losses. At one of the pre-battle conferences the question of using tanks to attack an unbroken gun line was raised by a commander who suggested it could lead to fifty per cent losses. He was told in no uncertain terms rocks, showering the men with lethal fragments which embedded in their skin and pierced vital organs. All these casualties were reliant on Henry and his colleagues to rescue them.

If Henry had thought the previous days were bad this was considerably worse. Even when they had successfully bought casualties back behind the lines they were not safe:

> What people do not realise is that if you are behind a tank battle, all the solid rounds which either cut clear through a tank, or miss, come bouncing across the desert. In the end we all took shelter in a slit trench, joined briefly by a couple of infantry men from 50 Division who during the battle had become detached from their battalion.
>
> At this moment a tank stopped to our rear, all pennants fluttering, the turret hatch opened and out popped the head of Monty, the 8th Army's commander. Oblivious to the cowering men in the slit trench, Monty began surveying the battle through his binoculars, and straight away his tank attracted fire from German Artillery. Two large black airbursts appeared as the Germans registered, showering us in the slit trench with shell fragments. This was too much for one rifleman who, turning towards his commanding General, told him in no uncertain terms to clear off. Monty's head disappeared inside as the tank backed away followed by another couple of airbursts.

But despite the heavy fighting and enormous casualties neither side made any real progress. Then at 11.00 the remains of the 15th Panzer, 21st Panzer and Littorio armoured divisions counter-attacked. But by that time the infantry had finally succeeded in digging in and a screen of anti-tank guns and artillery were in place. The counter-attack failed and Rommel lost 100 tanks.

For Henry the day seemed never ending. He was now as filthy as those who were fighting and his uniform was almost unrecognizable. His face was grey with dust, his throat hurt from smoke and the sand that swirled continuously round them, and his eyes were red rimmed and full of grit. He was deaf from the constant shelling and

that even if they sustained 100 per cent losses the objective must be gained.

Thus Operation Supercharge would begin with an infantry advance followed by an almost suicidal attack by an armoured brigade carrying out an infantry role. It was followed by the rest of the armoured brigades and infantry who would break out into the open desert. Here it was planned that the massed British armour would meet Rommel's Panzers and destroy them.

The assault began with 350 guns concentrating their bombardment on a 4,000-yard front with a shell landing approximately every twelve yards. After five minutes, a creeping barrage began which led the infantry in with strict instructions that they were not to stop for anything or anyone. As with Operation Lightfoot the wounded and dying were to be left for the stretcher bearers to deal with.

It was a very cold still night and in the brief pauses between the shelling Henry could again hear the solitary sound of a lone piper echoing eerily in the distance. Although he couldn't hear the tanks above the noise of the barrage, he could feel the ground vibrating as they crept slowly forward. He had no idea how they could see where they were going. Not only was it pitch black, the movement of the tanks and other vehicles were throwing up so many clouds of thick dust that visibility was severely impaired. He was standing some distance away but even here the dust from the tanks was swirling around in thick clouds, catching in his throat and making him cough.

Every so often when the dust cleared he could see burning vehicles. The light thrown up by the fires indicated they were probably the soft-skin ammunition lorries and petrol carriers of the infantry that were the victims of the enemy bombardment, not all of whom had been knocked out by the artillery barrage. As he watched he saw another flash and a big explosion and in the light from the subsequent fire he could just make out a tank swinging out to avoid the debris. When this happened he found himself holding his breath as invariably the tanks would find themselves in un-swept minefields. The explosions as they ran onto mines blew their tracks off, shattered the air and lit the sky and added to the cacophony of noise that swirled all around him. Once immobilised they were easy prey to the anti-tank guns.

Henry was right to be concerned. Of the seventy-nine Sherman and Grant tanks and fifty-three Crusader tanks that moved off from the concentration area only ninety-four took part in the attack. The rest were damaged and destroyed before reaching their objective. This confusion and delay meant that the whole forward momentum slowed, resulting in the 9th Armoured Brigade's attack to the Rahman track being delayed by half an hour: not an enormous amount of time but in this case a delay that meant the cover of darkness was gone and the armoured attack, suicidal at best, now had to take place in daylight.

As the sun rose he could just make out the fires across the other side of the track in the German areas. Then at 06.15 the real battle commenced as the tanks of the 9th Armoured Brigade went in under the bombardment.

Now that daylight had come Henry's view of the battle became clearer. Many of the gun positions appeared to be dug in on the reverse slopes of the slight inclines that undulated across the desert. The gunners waited until the tanks reared up to climb over the rise and then fired into the thinner metal of the underbelly. To his horror he watched as tank after tank 'brewed up'. The only sign in the distance was a ball of fire that indicated where once a tank had been. No mercy was given on either side as tank crews were gunned down by the enemy and gunners were shot as they tried to get away from the few tanks that had succeeded in breaking through. To Henry the whole scene was like something out of a picture he had once seen called 'Dante's Inferno'.

From the brigade start line to the Rahman Track there was complete devastation; a graveyard of tanks, guns and men. Gun barrels were sticking out of the sand at strange angles, burning tanks stood out in stark relief on the skyline and the wounded, dying and dead were scattered everywhere. The few still standing had uniforms grey with dust and sand. They were tattered, torn and blood splattered. Others were barely recognizable; their faces blackened by cordite and scarred by fire and their hands were filthy from oil and grease.

Everywhere he looked, tall, black clouds of smoke from the b[urning] tanks and other vehicles, rose into the air.

Time after time Henry and his fellow stretcher bearers [went] into this nightmare world. The wounded were never ending, [the] injuries so horrific that to start with Henry didn't know how he [was] going to be able to cope. But seeing the faces and hearing the [cries] of those he had come to help somehow gave him the courage [he] needed. Some were so badly burned or injured that he wa[s not] even sure if they were still alive but he knew he could not lea[ve] them there so he and his companions did the best they could. Ba[ck] they went again and again as the line of those waiting to see th[e] doctors grew longer and longer. After a while he no longer notice[d] the injuries and each casualty merged into the next until in hi[s] exhausted mind they all became one – a giant symbol of the horror of this desert war.

But the battle was not yet over. As the sun came up the German Panzer battalions moved slowly forward under a barrage of .88 shells. Against heavily-armed Panzers III and IV the British tanks were hopelessly outgunned, many only able to fire useless two-pounders.

The 9th Armoured Brigade started their attack with ninety-four tanks. Of these, only twenty-four were left; 230 men of the tank crews involved had been killed, captured or injured. Although they had caused considerable damage they had still failed to open a gap for the 1st Armoured Division to pass through. The battle raged on but by now the 1st Armoured Division had arrived and as the surviving tanks of the 9th joined them more reinforcements arrived in the form of the 2nd Armoured Brigade. Then, by mid-morning, the 8th Armoured Brigade also arrived. But while this was good news for the armoured brigades it was another story for the remaining infantry.

They now found themselves caught up in the open in the ferocious battle between the 1st Armoured Division and Rommel's dug-in Panzers and anti-tank guns. They couldn't dig in properly as once they reached 2ft they hit solid rock. The heavy shelling and mortaring were unceasing, relentlessly accurate and caused heavy casualties. Even the shells and mortar rounds that didn't make direct contact caused death and injury as they splintered the surrounding

the injuries of those he was rescuing no longer had the power to shock him. As he stumbled through the fine powdery sand of the track and across the hard barren rocks, his eyes were fixed firmly on a point on the horizon as he tried to identify the next place to go. His world had shrunk to the area on the battlefield in front of him and his only aim was to save those he'd been tasked to rescue and to somehow survive himself. Whilst their patient was the priority and they took every care to ensure he arrived back to the medical area still alive, they also had to look out for themselves.

The hardest part was the decisions as to who they should bring back and who they should leave. These often had to be made instantly. Quite simply they couldn't save everyone, so very early on they had realized that they had to have some way of prioritising the wounded. Some were almost dead anyway, others would clearly not survive the jolting of the stretcher as they ran crouching low across the desert with shells, mortars and machine-gun fire all around them. Several times they had to fling themselves into craters or behind the sandy inclines that littered the desert, to avoid the spray of a machine gun or a mortar that they instinctively knew were heading directly for them.

Those with limbs blown off or who were badly burnt would be least likely to survive. Although they knew basic first aid their knowledge was not always enough to stem arterial bleeding or prevent the severe dehydration caused by the burns. Although they risked their lives time and time again, gave water where they could, cigarettes to those who wanted them and even cradled the dying while the battle raged over their heads, Henry would never feel they had done enough and when the nightmares came later at least one would feature someone he'd left behind.

As dusk fell on 2 November Henry prayed that things would quieten down. But it was not to be. Despite having been under bombardment all day, the 7th Motor Brigade was now sent to capture the Rahman track along a two-mile front north of Tel el Aqaqir. The attack failed due to lack of time to reconnoitre the terrain in daylight and unexpectedly stiff resistance. For Henry and his fellow stretcher bearers, this meant more casualties, another never ending stream of wounded and dying: the victims of the strategic importance of a dirt

21

track in the middle of a desert. But Henry no longer had time to think about why they were fighting or even whether it was worth it as his whole being was firmly focused on how he could safely reach the next casualty.

After several long hours he was finally stood down and others took his place. Exhausted, he fell into a deep dreamless sleep and was so tired he was oblivious of the noise of the battle that continued to rage round him, leaving more dead and wounded in its wake.

The fighting continued throughout 3 November. The 1st Armoured Division were still unable to break through and the 2nd Armoured Brigade had been held by elements of the Afrika Korps and tanks of the Littorio Division. In the south, two German anti-tank battalions, who had been ordered forward to close a gap, suddenly came across the advancing 8th Armoured Brigade who was completely unaware of the German gunline. Behind the ridge the Ariete Division was holding its position but behind that the Germans and Italians were now beginning to withdraw.

On the evening of the 3 November Montgomery launched another attack at the Rahman Track, this time using three of the infantry brigades he had held in reserve.

The 5/7 Gordon Highlanders began their three-mile approach march at 15.00 across unswept minefields. But when they reached their forming-up point the tanks that were to accompany them were not there. Then information came in from 1st Armoured Division that the enemy were withdrawing so the air support and artillery barrage was cancelled. The Brigade HQ then suggested that the men ride on the outside of the tanks. Although the CO of 8RTR strenuously objected he was overruled.

So three platoons of Seaforth Highlanders were carried on the outside of the tanks as they advanced. But the intelligence had been wrong; the enemy were not withdrawing from that area. Instead 8RTR and the Seaforth Highlanders were advancing towards a gun-line of 88s attached to the 15th Panzer Division. They ran straight into the trap and six tanks were destroyed and eleven badly damaged in the first few moments. The Highlanders suffered terrible casualties with all the officers either wounded or killed in one company. The attack was halted while the survivors frantically dug in along the Rahman Track. The 5th Indian Brigade now joined the attack and, although their assault started off in equal confusion, it ended successfully. At last the enemy began to withdraw:

> The Germans finally began to withdraw on the night of 3 November but first they pinched all the Italian's transport and left their allies to be rounded up by 8th Army.

Despite being in amongst the heaviest fighting Henry had survived. He had also been promoted and was now a Lance Corporal. Looking around him he wondered what the future held. Although he'd been in amongst the thick of it and had survived some very close shaves, he still hadn't done any real fighting. But that would soon change.

Chapter 3

Preparation for War

Despite their defeat, the Panzerarmee Afrika had retained considerable strength. On 5 November the 15th Panzer still had eight tanks, 200 infantry, four anti-tank guns and twelve field guns although they did not have any 88mm left. The 21st Panzer Division had thirty tanks, 400 infantry, sixteen anti-tank guns and twenty-five field guns although, like the 15th Panzer, none were 88mm. The 164th Light Division had 600 officers and men of the 3 Panzergrenadier Battalion but no 88mm guns. They began retreating along the coast road; their vehicles often nose to tail which provided the RAF with excellent targets to bomb. They were closely followed by the 8th Army.

However the 8th Army now faced new challenges in its pursuit. The first problem was the acute congestion west of El Alamein caused by the extensive minefields that had not yet been cleared or at least cleared enough to make it safe. Thus hundreds of tanks and armoured cars of various divisions were caught up on the narrow corridor that had been swept, all competing for limited space and causing enormous traffic jams. Further congestion was caused by the thousands of Italian soldiers who had been abandoned by the Germans and who were frantically trying to surrender:

> You would see them sitting on the side of the road, many of the officers with suitcases waiting to put their hands up. Most seemed to be in a very bad way after the Germans had cleared off with their transport.

Although the Germans were also having problems it was not just a simple matter of the 8th Army catching up with them. They needed to first outflank them and then overtake. However, they couldn't follow on the coast road because it had been heavily mined and booby trapped by the retreating Germans. It took a long time to repair massive holes in the road so their only option was to swing south onto the open and much less congested desert. But the desert was heavily mined and driving across it had to be done using low gears. This used up a great deal of fuel, so as they attempted to outflank the Germans they began to run out of fuel. Whereas some of the fuel trucks were caught up in the massive traffic congestion, others were two-wheel-drive vehicles which made them prone to getting stuck in the sand. As the tanks and armoured cars churned up the sand, the terrain became even more difficult for these fuel lorries to negotiate.

They were further delayed by the extensive minefields. The Germans had used booby-trapped aerial bombs which meant retraining the sappers so they could defuse different types of bombs. They had also booby trapped numerous other items including empty tins, abandoned kit and burnt-out vehicles. This made it extremely dangerous to come into contact with anything that had been left behind. Even dead bodies had been booby trapped which meant further delay as grappling hooks fixed to lengths of reinforced bars and cables had to be used to pull the decomposing bodies out of the way of the advancing troops.

Despite these problems they initially made good progress; XIII Corps took 6,000 prisoners on 5 November and by 7 November the 2nd New Zealand Division had reached the coast road by Fuka. The 22nd Armoured Brigade had reached just south of Mersa Matruh and was not far behind the 21st Panzer by 6 November, but then they ran out of fuel. The 2nd Armoured Brigade also ran out of fuel on 6 November and had to wait over twenty-four hours for fresh supplies. Despite this, between 4 and 17 November over 17,000 German and Italian prisoners were taken and the chase continued until the weather turned:

> The pursuit of the Germans carried on until the rains in late November turned the desert into a lake which was almost impassable to vehicles.

Although the desert was searing hot from May to October, from November to April there were infrequent flash floods which made the roads virtually impassable. These rains began on 6 November and by late November it was impossible to push forward any further so the pursuit of the retreating Axis armies stopped.

The rain was torrential and continued for days without a break. The desert with its fine, powdery sand that clogged everything up was transformed almost overnight into an impassable swamp. The swirling dust clouds were now replaced by thick mist and fog which reduced visibility even more than the dust had. Everything was covered in a thick film of mud including clothes and boots. The advance finally came to a standstill as tanks, armoured vehicles and fuel lorries were sucked into a boggy sea of sandy mud. Having ground to a halt, 8th Army used the time to carry out repairs and refits, undergo re-training and generally prepare for the next offensive, once the weather improved:

> The battalion stopped at Mursa Matruh to undertake repairs and sort out the new riflemen into their companies. Now came the splitting up of my draft to fill the holes left in the battalions after Alamein. I found myself with the 7th Battalion (7RB) again, Territorials of the London Rifle Brigade, most pre-war soldiers and veterans of the First and Second Battles of Alamein. Most of my draft was made up of Londoners, men from the building trade, many of whom had endured the Blitz only to be conscripted in 1941. Their experiences of the bombing of London in the autumn of 1940 had toughened their attitude towards the Germans.

Henry had no trouble fitting in with these men whose backgrounds were similar to his own. Born on 6 April 1922 he was the first son, although not the first child, of Henry Charles and Daisy Taylor. The family home was on Southbury Road, Ponders End, a working-class area of Enfield in Middlesex. Born in the years of financial hardship after the First World War, families were large so that when the children reached school-leaving age they could work to add to the household income. Women had by then returned to

27

their traditional role of home-maker, ruling the house with a rod of iron and demanding a proportion of the wages brought home, first by their husbands and then their children.

Many of the men endured hard back-breaking manual work after having given the best years of their lives serving King and Country in the Great War as the First World War was known. Henry took his own father's name, Henry Charles Taylor, adding junior as he grew older to prevent confusion. His father had been a sailor in the Great War and was a man of immense stature from his days as a stoker in the King's Navy. On leaving the service after the Great War he was employed in the same job at Brimsdown power station in Enfield and to earn a little more money as his family grew, he ran a pig farm on waste ground. In true Victorian working-class fashion his mother toiled at home. To add to the family finances she took in extra washing, scrubbed out other people's homes, and on occasions laid out the dead in their own homes. It was this Dickensian world that shaped Henry's attitude to life.

At the age of five he started the same school that his father had attended. Classes then were very large by today's standards with forty-four boys crammed into a room. The teacher was invariably an ex-serviceman whose idea of discipline had changed little from the trenches. School life in the early 1920s consisted of learning lessons by rote, reading, writing and arithmetic, with children coming to school in hand-me-down clothes and many without shoes. Receiving the cane from the Headmaster as punishment was common place and, needless to say, Henry received his fair share:

> Most of the time we got the cane on the hands – nine of the best we called it – for anything; if you had more than one tool on the desk in woodwork, ink blots on your work, or in my case were fighting in the playground. Canes did go missing. Later when a display case of sporting cups was moved dozens of canes were found behind it!

Although Henry considered that most of his actions did not warrant the cane there was one incident that even he thought was probably deserving of the punishment:

28

One of my teachers owned a motor bike and side car. He parked it under the window of the staffroom so as to keep an eye on it. One dinnertime me and a mate of mine decided to go for a ride. We started it up and rode it around to the back of the school. Who should be looking out the window but this particular teacher, so as I was doing the driving I headed for the bike shed forgetting the iron stanchion holding up the roof. I went one side and my mate in the side car went the other. You can imagine what happened! There was an almighty crash and the bike and side car parted company. We thought the sky had fallen down on us. We certainly did deserve the thrashing we got, and in front of the school to boot.

Sport became a welcome release from the unremitting grind of daily life. Henry was a keen boxing fan and when he was old enough he joined a boxing club. The local Ponders End boxing club was run by an old bare-knuckle fighter who in his later years sparred with some of the great boxers of his age. Local boys enrolled and were taught the basics of the noble art. After training they would all crowd into the old fighter's office to look at his mementos collected over the years:

> Among the posters and medals was a pair of gloves worn by Sam Langford, the black heavyweight boxer who got into the ring with the Great Jack Johnson. The gloves were a present from Langford to the old boy who ran the club for his hours of sparring.

Another popular pastime in the winter was football and this was something that Henry really enjoyed:

> Our school team was the best in Enfield and we thrashed all comers. A couple of the lads went on to play for Spurs and we even took on West Ham school boys. Nearly all the team went into the forces during the war, few returned.

29

In summer football was replaced with athletics which gave Henry another chance to shine.

> I joined Ponders End Athletic Club. Most races took place at fêtes and these attracted some of the best runners of the time. The races were handicaps and all ages competed. I was a hundred-yard runner and took some catching. My grandfather was a famous amateur marathon runner and he took an interest in me, so much so I did run for Middlesex.

Although sport kept Henry out of trouble most of the time, he did find himself playing the same pranks as most boys of his age including scrumping (stealing apples) from the numerous orchards which surrounded Ponders End at the time, or missing school and hiding in his mother's rabbit hutch. However one particular game gave him the biggest thrill:

> We grew up with stories of the Great War. The local flea pit (cinema) showed all the films from the war and my particular favourite was *Hill 60*. When the mine went off on the screen, a bloke fired a blank from a pistol, and all the audience jumped!
>
> To recreate these war-time films, each street in Ponders End had a gang of boys whose job it was to raid the other streets in the area and take one of their boys as prisoner. We then defended our street when the other street's gang came to get him back. Sometimes we went further afield and raided Enfield Highway or Enfield Lock, two of the toughest areas in Enfield. For an attack on Enfield Lock we always tested ourselves against the boys from Alma Road. On these occasions we went armed with broom handles and dustbin lids. There were a couple of bombsites near to Alma Road on which were dug a few trenches, and we Southbury Road boys organized trench raids against Alma Road. Getting back with a prisoner was a problem as we had to frogmarch him through all the other streets and all

30

the while watching for the Alma Road boys on our tails. All this larking about came in handy during the war.

As his family grew, Henry came under more pressure to leave school and find work, so a few days short of his fourteenth birthday he left school:

> My father found me a job in the brick field – my Grand-father worked here so he could keep an eye on me. I did attain a good education for the time and was able to read, write and add up. In these times every child learnt the meaning of what it meant to be British. We had a huge map of the world in the classroom showing the pink of the British Empire and everyone stood and sung the national anthem on Empire day. Although most people did not have two pennies to rub together, they were all proud to be part of what the British Empire stood for.

Gradually the economy began to turn round and after the Great Depression things began to ease a little. Henry began to enjoy regular trips to Southend or Clacton, the charabanc leaving Southbury Road early in the morning with everyone in their Sunday best. But it was now the 1930s and already the storm clouds were gathering once again over Europe:

> I worked with a fair few old soldiers and sailors in the brickfields. All saw the warning signs coming from Germany but most of the country still steadfastly chose to ignore the threat and continued to stick their heads in the sand. My father would argue with people who thought Winston Churchill a war monger. His speeches were daily ridiculed in the papers and ignored in parliament. By now I was earning a man's wage and enjoying the perks of a few bob to go dancing up the posh end of Enfield with the girls in service around Enfield Town. I half listened to the old soldiers and thought old Adolf was not going to spoil my nights out with another war.

31

In the meantime life went on. Work in the brickfield was seasonal so in the cold winter months Henry worked in the factories which gave employment to many in Enfield. Not wishing to stay a labourer all his life, he decided to sign on as an apprentice bricklayer working for a local building firm:

> Competition among tradesmen in the mid thirties was intense, so for a youngster like myself just starting out life was difficult. The foreman at the firm taught me the hard way, going through every step from knocking up the mortar, hod carrying and finally picking up a trowel and lines. Laying bricks is not easy. First you get the corners up and make sure they're square, then you fill in between, and woe betide if the finished wall was even half an inch out of upright. Then I had to take the wall down, clean the bricks, and start again. On one occasion I was still on the site at nine at night.

This attention to detail and pride in his work stayed with Henry all his life and played a significant part of his time in the army.

By now the situation in Europe was rapidly deteriorating and when Prime Minister Neville Chamberlain returned from his meeting with Hitler and proclaimed 'peace in our time', Henry remembered the country's relief that their prime minister had averted another war. The chance of a repeat of the Battle of the Somme and of Paschendale now seemed unlikely and the papers and radio broadcasts were full of 'peace in our time'. But despite this there was an increased call for underground shelters to be built which meant that Henry, with his new trade, had plenty of work:

> I now realise that the brick and concrete shelters we built all over the place in 1938 were in preparation for war. Most days I was up at 4.30. Mum had my breakfast ready and then it was off on my push bike to all kinds of places in Enfield and the surrounding countryside. I remember the bike. It had belonged to a Belgian postman who had been

evacuated in 1914 and somehow came into my father's possession. Its brakes were dodgy and on more than one occasion I found myself thrown over the handle bars.

We started digging Anderson shelters, ARP huts and the like, and then we began building concrete bases for Nissan huts. Oh, the country knew what was coming all right. I can remember where I was when the balloon went up – I was building an ARP shelter near Oakwood tube station. Next minute all the air-raid sirens went off and people scurried around looking at the sky and diving down the underground. Don't know what they expected to see, but all this put paid to my dancing at night for a while.

Henry spent the winter of 1939 back at his various factory jobs and the nights as part of the firm's fire watchers. The winter was bitterly cold – one of the coldest on record – and only reports of patrol action by the British Expeditionary Force (BEF) in France and the action at sea proved that Britain was in fact at war with Germany:

> The navy was busy which pleased my father. The sinking of the *Graf Spey* cheered everyone up, then HMS *Cossack* chased the *Altmark* down a fjord and released some of our sailors. There was no rationing to speak of although the women started queuing for some essentials. Life was normal. I went dancing on my days off from fire-watching, although the blackout meant you had to watch the few cars in case they ran you over. Everywhere people were digging and sandbagging buildings, but we all thought the war would be over soon, except that is the blokes who had fought in the last war.

The spring of 1940 saw an increase in digging of trenches and defences as building of camps and other fortifications all over Britain continued. Henry, like most people, still thought the war would soon be over but continued to prepare:

There is nothing like being prepared. The Luftwaffe started flying over and photographing targets up north. Our fighters were after German recce aircraft and reports of increased activity on the Dutch/German border filled the front of the papers and the radio. Still, everyone was confident; everyone knew the German tanks were made of cardboard and that we and the French would be a different kettle of fish to the Poles. *Pathe News* poked fun at the Germans and it would only be a matter of time before we would hang out the washing on the Siegfried Line. Spring turned into the warm summer of 1940 and all hell broke loose over in Belgium.

As the BEF advanced from its defences into France the old soldiers from the last war began to take even more notice of the news reports. Some went off to join the Local Defence Volunteers, while other signed up with the Civil Defence. As a Fire Guard I was issued with a bucket to fill with sand in case of incendiaries.

Things on the continent rapidly deteriorated. As the Anglo-French armies were drawn forward into Belgium by the first part of the German attack, they were effectively cut off from their supply bases by another attack from the Panzer divisions through Sedan. Now it was only a matter of time before the Anglo-French armies were surrounded and destroyed:

Things looked dead dodgy for the army in France and the old soldiers from the last war shook their heads in disbelief as one town after another fell to the Germans. Most knew that once Sedan fell to the Germans things would rapidly get bad. Some of the first wounded arrived soon after the fighting started with North Middlesex and Chase Farm Hospitals taking men from all three services and reverting to the role they had in the Great War.

The evacuation of the army from Dunkirk was a shock. My foreman was an old soldier from the last war and he

34

had tears in his eyes one morning. We asked him what was up. He shook his head and told us he had seen hundreds of our soldiers sitting forlornly along the Great Cambridge Road. Apparently the trains picked them up from Dover and dumped them in Enfield. Everyone now expected the invasion to follow and so efforts to prepare went on at a pace. The Germans finished off what was left of the French army and then started attacking convoys in the channel and shelling Dover.

As June and July slipped past the fear of invasion grew and then, in August, the Battle of Britain began and Henry had a ring-side seat:

It seemed to be hot and sunny every day with not a cloud in the sky. You could have your tea break and watch the air battles thousands of feet above your head. The Germans came over like clockwork after the RAF fighter air fields around London. One day we were digging drainage ditches and they bombed Hatfield. About ten Heinkels came skating along at tree-top height with Spitfires after them. One Spitfire caught up with this Heinkel right over the top of us. He let fly with all his guns and we got the over throws on the ground. Good job we were all in a trench. The newspapers next day said that the Spitfires brought down every one of the German bombers before they reached the coast.

As the 'few' fought the many and the Luftwaffe failed to destroy RAF Fighter Command they began to switch to the bombing of London:

Every day the bombing got nearer with raids on Kent, Sussex and Surrey, and then one day they hit the outskirts of London. Standing on the Ridgeway in Enfield at night you could see London alight; a red glow which faded then

35

grew as bombs ignited. Enfield now came in for its fair share.

As shipping losses at sea began to mount, the government led by Winston Churchill, brought in more rationing. The campaign in Norway which had begun before the Battle of France was going badly so things looked bleak on all fronts. To help the war effort, the people of Britain rolled their sleeves up and began to settle in for a long conflict. Henry was now busier than ever:

> But all my time now was taken up with the building of even more shelters and being on fire guard at night. I still went dancing but on many occasion I found myself doing fire watching in my best whistle.[1]
>
> On one particular night during the height of the Blitz I was on duty with my individual buckets of sand and water. The anti-aircraft guns were putting up a right old barrage and lumps of shell fragments were falling on the roofs of houses. People don't realise that everything that goes up comes down. So not only were we looking out for German bombs and incendiaries but also bits from our own anti-aircraft shells. I stood in a door way to find a bit of shelter when a shell fragment hit my shoulder and ripped the sleeve from my coat. I escaped without a scratch, but it buggered my suit up.
>
> After a raid I spent the day doing bomb damage work. This meant going through the rubble to look for survivors, making the buildings safe and then clearing away the debris from the streets. In one raid a land mine as we called them, destroyed the Catholic Church in Enfield Town and killed or wounded people who had been leaving the cinema opposite. When we arrived the next morning there were still arms and other bits and pieces laying around. One woman had her face blown off by the blast which killed her boyfriend. We set to work digging into what remained of the church and soon found the only casualties – a man and woman in each others' arms, killed instantly by the blast.

36

In the dark days of 1940 and 1941 Henry's skills as a bricklayer were very much in demand. As the size of the army increased additional camps were needed to house them:

> Another job we had was building concrete bases for Nissan huts because the army might requisition land for a camp then need the huts built. On this occasion, the land was near to a RAF secondary field used to land fighters if North Weald was under attack.
>
> We started at first light in the summer so I got up at four in the morning and cycled there on my Belgian bike. All this work and exercise meant I was very thin for my 6ft height. I was like a rake and weighed 10st 2lb. Anyway we got these bases down in no time and put up the huts ready for a battalion of the Duke of Cornwall's Light Infantry. They in turn dished out some of the spare rations so we all got on like a house on fire.
>
> It did not last. One morning we arrived and the camp had been hit by an air raid and a good few of the huts were in bits. What remained of the squaddies was scattered all over the place. Our foreman detailed us off to pick the bits up and to collect what remained of some of the blokes up in the trees. I tell you one thing; it did harden me up no end.

Note

1. A 'Whistle' is cockney rhyming slang for a suit.

Chapter 4

Ambush

The fighting had ceased and the 8th Army settled down for the winter, waiting for the weather to improve. But here was still work to be done:

> Every rifleman was expected to be able to do maintenance on vehicles and we got to work on these tasks at once. Later some of the men had a scout around the area and discovered an old Italian supply dump. There were literally thousands of small tins lying around in the sand and we initially thought they were tins of hair cream. We opened them up and smeared the contents on our hair. It was not until later that an old desert hand informed us that the tins contained anti-mosquito cream! It did the trick and we were not bothered by the insect for weeks. It was here that the battalion received its new commanding officer, Major Douglas Darling, a regular officer, a first at Sandhurst and a veteran of the 2nd battalion. The first task of our new Commanding Officer was to send down to base for barbers as the battalion had not had a haircut since well before Alamein.
>
> Lieutenant Colonel Douglas Darling commanded the battalion from 1942 after the Battle of Alamein. A pre-war regular soldier he won the Sword of Honour as an officer cadet at Sandhurst. As a junior officer he served with 2RB at the outbreak of war in the desert, fighting with them in the early battles of the North African campaign. Promoted

to Major he then moved to the staff of XX Corps during the Battles of Alamein.

When Major Darling took over 7RB any officers not coming up to scratch were removed. He considered us his rifleman and only the best would do. The battalion was made up mainly of Londoners so nicknames were the order of the day. One officer in particular complained that his men called him 'Fishy' (the officer's name being Eales). Darling replied that this particular officer should not worry; the men knew their commanding officer as 'Bombhead'. This nickname was due to his aggressive style of command which on a few occasions landed the battalion in a few scrapes. However this did not prevent us keeping the Germans on the move most of the time.

Going around hellfire pass was dead dodgy after Alamein as there are a succession of hairpin bends and if you are driving a carrier as I was then it is double dodgy.

What you have to do is go up to the bend and then reverse back and forth until the nose of the carrier is around the corner and all the time with a shear drop behind and to the side of you. If this is not bad enough, then try it when you are being attacked by aircraft.

The Germans must have had an airfield at the top or near as damn it, for all the time we were under attack by JU 88s and Stukas. These would waddle into the air, circle around a bit then swoop down and drop their bombs on all the traffic backed up on the hairpin bends. I don't know how they missed, but they did hit a 25-pounder and Quad further up which came bouncing down narrowly missing a couple of carriers behind me. After they had caused all this pandemonium the German aircraft landed on their airfield, loaded up with bombs, and did the same again.

During the night the heat went and we soon shivered as the temperatures began to drop. The night-time desert sky was full of stars; the aurora borealis shone down as we slept out in the open under a blanket. Sometimes a frost would come down. Many of the blokes slept in their great coats

40

and we were all covered in dew by the morning but this came in handy. We washed our clothes in petrol to save water and kill any 'lodgers' as we called the lice. When we had done, the clothes were laid out over scrub or on a line hooked over the vehicles. The petrol then evaporated and most of the time the dew was useful in getting rid of the smell. When the sun came up the heat soon dried off the clothes and we put them on. Some of the blokes would then light a fag but none of them caught fire!

Then we had to contend with the sandstorms. One in particular I remember lasted for three whole days and if this was not bad enough, there was the Khams Inés, a hot wind which the locals said would drive a white man mad. They weren't far wrong; we all must have been a bit off our rockers fighting in all this.

When the stars weren't shining it was so dark in the desert that it was easy to get lost when leaving a slit trench or a tent to use the latrine. Soldiers were either advised to take a compass bearing or tie a cord to a peg in the ground by the trench and play it out to the latrine, thus leaving a guide to the way back:

Eating in the desert was a bind because of the flies. As soon as you opened a tin of bully (corned beef) the flies would swarm all over the food. Because of the heat, the contents of the tin were poured out like a stew and then spread on army biscuits. We did get some bacon which we fried in a mess tin over our Jhildi brewers – petrol cans with the top third cut off and half filled with sand on to which petrol was poured. The petrol soaked into the sand and you could then put a match to it and get a good flame for cooking. We soaked the army biscuits in the fat from what the army jokingly called bacon. We also boiled water for tea; our ration was a pint and a half per day for washing, shaving and of course a brew up. Some officer calculated that every stop in the desert cost 8th Army 52,000 gallons of petrol when the blokes used their Jhildi brewers to make tea.

41

Before Alamein, the 8th Army had reorganized and broken up the 9th Battalion of the Rifle Brigade (1st Battalion Tower Hamlet Rifles) as reinforcements for the other Rifle Brigade battalions. Known to everyone as the 'Benghazi Harriers' because of their exploits up and down the desert when Rommel first appeared in 1941, the blokes from 9RB were experienced desert hands and those who joined our battalion taught us all the wrinkles of desert life. One old sweat came to our battalion as a corporal and brought with him a good way of getting rid of the flies. When we stopped for connor (food), this corporal would take his boots off and change his socks. He had a fungal infection between his toes and his feet and socks stunk to high heaven. We would tell him to go and hang his socks off one of the vehicles and this in many cases attracted enough flies for us to eat our grub in peace.

On some occasions when we stopped miles from any-where there would be no hint of human habitation, only a forty-gallon drum as a navigation mark. As we started to get ourselves organized, up would come an Arab on a donkey. Where he came from no one knew. He would offer us small eggs which usually cost a few ackers, but sometimes these blokes might barter the eggs for some tea or fags – although if you offered him Victory V cigarettes then he would shake his head and say 'Those shit Johnny'. The VVs were indeed awful. After a time we were told not to let these Arabs anywhere near us as the army said that most were spying for the Germans.

Infection was a problem in the desert. Most of the old hands told us youngsters not to wear shorts as any loss of bark from knees led to festering desert sores and so we all invested in long trousers. Most of the old desert hands were plagued by these sores; any exposed area which you knocked was soon covered by weeping sores. Any occasion we stopped for a rest near the coast the blokes would go for a swim in the sea and let the salt disinfect the sores and the fish nip the tops from the scabs.

42

Long experience of fighting in the desert had taught the British Army that strict hygiene precautions were of the utmost importance. Latrines in the desert consisted of a deep hole into which a bottomless empty petrol tin was placed vertically. Another was placed at an angle and this was frequently disinfected with chloride. In static areas the latrines were sturdier and consisted of a hessian screen stretched on poles across a deep trench, but the frequency of disinfection did not vary as dysentery and other fly borne plagues were an ongoing danger:

> The army tried to cut down on all infections. We used the 'Desert Rose' as a latrine. This was a bucket which was burnt out after everyone was finished, and all waste had to be buried. The MO came round with our malaria tablets and stood in front of us to make sure we took them. He had learnt from experience. These tablets were a pinkish colour and tasted horrible. The blokes more often than not spat them out and then swore blind to the MO they had taken them. He believed us until the dew came down that night and the moisture caused the pills to dissolve. Next morning the sand in the company area had turned a shade of pink.
>
> As motor battalions we were self-contained. When our battalion moved in the desert it looked like a travelling circus. All manner of things hung from the outside of the vehicles while all the internal storage was given over to water, petrol and ammo. Everyone could drive, maintain vehicles, and to some extent navigate in the desert using the stars and compass. After Alamein I was in one of the motor platoons driving a Bren gun carrier. On halts my job was to maintain the three carriers in the section.
>
> The desert was unforgiving on moving parts. Engines would need replacing on a regular basis; oil filters would soon fill with sand, tracks would wear out and the hard jelly lubricant would run from the carrier's bogeys. Every now and again we would take a couple of three-toners and do a run to the coast to pick up water. Further up the desert this

was supplied by the navy who brought it up in forty-gallon drums and dropped them off to be brought ashore on boats. In Cyrenaica we tried using wells sunk by the Italians but some were polluted with dead bodies left by the retreating Germans, while others had a film of oil over the surface. Little did we know then the oil was seeping into the well.

The motor battalions' self-sufficiency now came in very handy. Driving a 15-cwt, some of us were on a long run back to pick up spares and other essentials. We had a corporal in charge who was convinced we would hit a mine and told us so as we drove back along the track towards 8th Army. Well, would you know it? With the entire desert around us and about half way, we *did* hit a mine.

'I told you so,' the corporal shouted as we watched one of the front wheels cartwheel across the desert and then felt the truck nose dive into the sand. A dozy Italian engineer had laid a few anti-tank mines and we had hit one a glancing blow. We were now stranded in the desert with our water running low, and traffic on this particular track was scarce. Luckily we now considered ourselves old hands and settled down to wait next for the truck. As the sun set, the corporal spotted another vehicle in the distance and asked for volunteers to go and see if it still had water in its radiator. So off I went with another rifleman with canteens.

Anyone who fought in the desert will tell you that distances can be deceptive so what looked like only a short stroll turned into a route march. As the night came on, we took a star fix and stumbled onto the wreck some hours later. The lorry was German and with usual efficiency they had topped the rad up with water, so we drained the liquid into the canteens and then set off on our return journey, trusting on the star fix.

We made our way back and handed the canteens over to the corporal who, sipping the water, declared it was tainted with anti-freeze. That's German efficiency for you. Anyway this water kept us going for a couple of days until we were picked up by another 15-cwt from our battalion looking for

44

us. We had survived our time in the desert but I shudder to think what the water from that German lorry's radiator did to our insides.

As the 8th Army closed on up to the old French defences on the borders of Tunisia, preparations were made to storm the German and Italian defences on the Mareth Line. It was decided that three divisions would be sent on a left hook around the open edge of the defences, while the rest of 8th Army mounted a frontal assault on the Mareth Line. These three divisions would support the Anglo American 1st Army already fighting in the hills of Tunisia. It was the day before my twenty-first birthday when we headed towards the Mareth Line in the back of the lorry. As I looked out across the desert, the sun was sinking slowly into the horizon and the sky was blood red.

The US 2nd Corps and the British 1st Army had landed in French North Africa in November 1942 and had initially made good progress, reaching the north coastal area of Tunisia by mid November and occupying the town of Tebourba. However, the Germans then counter-attacked, driving them out of the town and halting the advance. Heavy rains in December prevented any real advances and both armies had settled down to over winter.

In mid February 1943 the 7th Armoured Division led the 8th Army into Tunisia and by 20 February they had taken Tataouine and Medenine. From here Monty planned his attack on the Mareth Line which extended from the sea to a point twelve miles inland in the Matmata Hills. It had been built in the 1930s by the French to protect Tunisia from the Italians. The defences consisted of a system of deep trenches and block houses each designed to give covering fire if the one nearest it was hit. In front of the defensive positions was a deep and wide wadi which acted as a natural anti-tank ditch. In front of this were fields of mines and barbed wire entanglements which had been placed there over several weeks. However Rommel was not over impressed by the Mareth Line, considering it dilapidated and easily outflanked. Rather than leave himself open to defeat, he withdrew his troops into Tunisia and dug in at Gabes Gap, a much shorter and more easily defended position line slightly east of the Mareth Line.

This first attack on the Mareth Line initially met little resistance, as on 14 February Rommel had turned his attention to the US 2nd Corps who were advancing at Kasserine. The US II Army and the British 1st Army were now taught the lessons of desert warfare that the 8th Army had already painfully learned during the past two years. Rommel's counter-attack became so serious that it began to threaten the Allied advance so command changes were made. All allied forces in North Africa, the 8th Army, 1st Army and American Forces, were now combined and renamed 18th Army Group with General Alexander in overall command.

To relieve pressure on the US II Corps General Alexander immediately sent a message to Monty asking him to attack the enemy on the Mareth Line so that Rommel would have to withdraw some of his forces from Kasserine. Fortunately this tactic worked and by the end of February the Panzer Army Afrika began withdrawing in the face of attacks from the 1st Army in the west and the 8th Army in the south.

Rommel now launched a new attack on the 8th Army at Medenine on 6 March and 160 Axis tanks advanced cautiously forward under cover of thick fog. Although the 8th Army heard them coming they did nothing until the sun came up and then the anti-tank guns opened up, catching numerous tanks out in open ground. Three times the Panzers withdrew, regrouped and advanced, but each time they were met with a hail of fire by the anti-tank guns. By the afternoon Rommel had lost fifty tanks and the British had lost none:

> By early 1943 all preparations were completed. Now, 7RB along with the other rifle battalions, were under command of 7th Armoured Division and moved off towards the rear of the Axis defences. On our journey the battalion was attacked by German aircraft. The Luftwaffe was still very active and was giving as good as it got, and on this occasion our visitors were Me 109s. One in particular pressed his attack home with machine guns and bombs. I was now driving a Bren gun carrier in one of the motor platoons and

had one of their company cooks as an extra passenger. Without orders, the cook, who was known as Chalky White, took on the 109 with a Bren gun and knocked it down. The plane hit the ground full out and broke up at once. Chalky's burst from the Bren must have killed the pilot and everyone gave him a huge cheer. However, Chalky soon found himself in trouble for firing without orders. Needless to say he got away with a telling off.

Chalky wasn't the only one who found himself in trouble in the months after El Alamein. Henry, only recently promoted, now lost his Corporal stripes after finding one of the men stealing water. Stealing was one thing that was never tolerated, so after several moments of confrontation and lack of contrition, Henry hit him, resulting in the loss of his hard won stripes. Although he considered this to be unfair there was little he could do about it so he soon forgot about it. There were many more important things to be worrying about, not least the next assault which was now being planned.

By the middle of March the US II Corps was ready to go on the offensive again and on 17 March the American II Corps under General Patton reopened the attack in the mountains of Tunisia. Three days later, on 20 March, the 8th Army attacked the Mareth Line. By 23 March, after three days of heavy fighting, they had broken through and the Germans had withdrawn to Wadi Akerit and the Gabes Gap. After months of desperately requesting reinforcements, the Herman Goring Division now arrived by air to reinforce the German position and the Germans dug in as they waited for the next assault.

The place Rommel had chosen for his next stand was the last natural barrier barring the way from the south to Tunisia's coastal plain. Although it was chosen because of its natural advantages over the Mareth Line, it did however, lack defensive depth and extensive field works. Stretching eighteen miles inland from the sea to Djebel Haidoudi in the west, the British called it the Akarit Line because of the deep, wide Wadi Akarit which stretched four miles inland from the coast. The Germans called it the Chott Line because the

47

western edge was on the great salt marsh of Chott El-Fedjadi, which could only be crossed once the winter rains and flooding had dried out sufficiently to allow vehicles to pass.

The coastal sector itself was dominated by two main features. To the east was Djebel Roumana, a 500ft-high, bare, steep-sided ridge that ran virtually parallel to the coast and was impassable to both wheeled and tracked vehicles. To the west of the ridge the ground started off fairly level but then gradually became undulating. At its western edge was the Djebel Tebaga Fatnassa. This was a complicated maze of steep-sided hills, cliffs, escarpments, gullies and peaks with twisting narrow valleys and corridors between them and dominated by a 900ft conical hill called Zovai.

The west of Fatnassa was protected by the Djebel Zemlet El-Beida hills which were 500ft high and ran south-west towards Djebel Haidoudi which itself overlooked the metal road linking Gabes and El-Guettar and Gafsa.

The Germans had strengthened the sides of the Wadi Akarit by steepening them and had extended it to Roumana by means of an anti-tank ditch. They had dug another deep ditch from Roumana to Fatnassa and planted up to 4,000 mines between the coastal road and Roumana and in the countryside between Roumana and Fatnassa. There were also several barbed wire entanglements.

On 6 April the 8th Army broke through the Gabes Gap and began to pursue the Germans north towards Tunis. Henry was now back with 7th Motor Brigade, 1st Armoured Division:

> The battalion's first action in Tunisia was Gabes Gap or the Akarit Line. A&B companies were tasked to clear the enemy from objectives, which were taken with little fuss. An officer then fired a success flare and all hell broke loose. We had jabbed into the German rear and attracted one of its reserve divisions, the 21st Panzer Division. In the space of one-and-a-half hours the battalion felt the full weight of the Panzer Division's fire power. Vehicles began to catch fire and explode and the battalion's porters carrying our six-pounder anti-tank guns were all knocked out, so there was nothing for it but to withdraw. Our line of retreat was

across the front of a salt marsh and we were chased all the way by accurate artillery fire. At no time had we even seen a German.

Our losses amounted to twenty-two officers and 480 men killed, wounded or missing. Not to be down hearted, Major Darling proposed a second attack with a few replacements found from somewhere. But this was called off and the battalion settled down to lick its wounds at El Hamma.

Right on cue the battalion area was attacked again by the Luftwaffe, this time FW 190s, whose bombs killed two men from another Bren gun carrier. Together with Freddie Arnold, another Bren gun carrier driver, we had to recover the remains of one man. The force of the blast had blown him through the vehicle's wheels, dissecting him in four. He had lots of sores on his arms which were covered in bandages and these had wrapped themselves round the spikes in the wheels. It took over an hour to get all of him out. We buried him and played the Last Post. I never liked it after that as every time I heard it all I could think of was that burial in the desert.

On the whole though, the attack at Gabes was a success. The hole made in the German defences had allowed 4th Indian Division to exploit the gap. And the officer who fired the flare? He left the battalion forthwith.

Our next waltz with the Germans was at Djebel Kournine. Most of the missing and walking wounded had returned so the battalion was at near full strength. Changes had taken place with our equipment so now the Bren carriers towed the six-pounders. Before we arrived an action had been fought by one of our armoured regiments at Argoub el Megas against a force of German Tiger tanks. The remains of knocked-out Shermans littered the area. A Bren carrier had tried to take out some of the wounded Tanki Wallahs but this too had fallen victim to the Tigers and its burnt-out hulk contained the remains of the wounded. In an attempt to deal with the Tigers, some of the brewed-up Shermans were replaced at night with new vehicles. This did not fool the Germans who dealt with these Shermans at first light.

Our CO ordered a thorough recce of the area before he committed the battalion into this cauldron. An officer and two riflemen crept out into 'no man's land' and reported the Tigers had gone. The battalion advanced at last light and ran straight into the Tigers, now supported by a company of infantry. Our route took us through a series of wadis which were now cultivated and covered with ripening corn. It was meant to be a silent attack and I drove one of the lead Bren carriers pulling a six-pounder, along with the gun's crew.

The Germans caught us in a very well planned ambush. They filled a small farm hut with petrol and with our appearance set the hut alight with tracer. With the corn field well alight, and as night turned to day, the Tigers opened fire.

Chapter 5

My Fourth Bren Gun Carrier in a Day

In the glow of the burning corn these Tigers looked the size of a London bus and their guns the length of telegraph poles. If this was not bad enough, their infantry support was well dug in. The 6-pounder crew jumped off my carrier, unhitched the gun and brought it into action. At this short range they could not miss the nearest Tiger and at about seventy yards their first round hit it. I think the Germans were really surprised how fast the six-pounder came into action and they bailed out of their Tiger double quick. The crew did not have long to enjoy their success as a second Tiger hit the gun with a H.E. round, knocked it out and killed them.

While all this was going on, my gunner was taking on a third Tiger with a .05 Browning machine gun. It had no effect and the red hot cartridges were spraying all over me in the driver's position. We had certainly got this Tiger's attention. The turret traversed following the tracer rounds from the Browning and put a solid armour piercing round through the front of my carrier and took the engine clear out of the back.

The flame from the gun seemed to touch the end of my nose and the jolt moved the carrier back a dozen feet and knocked my knees out of joint. Petrol from the remains of the fuel tank ignited and the carrier burst into flames. This persuaded me to get out and join the shambles going on around me but with my knees out of joint I could not get out of the driver's seat. Luckily my gunner, a chap named Horace Kinney, grabbed me under the arms and yanked me out. One of our platoons was then ordered to fix swords (bayonets) and charge the German infantry protecting the tanks. An argument between the officer and the riflemen broke out as the riflemen refused to undertake such a suicidal attack. The officer gave one final order to which he got the reply 'Bollocks' and the attack was called off.

Although in some pain, I was ordered to find another carrier and with all the abandoned ones lying about I had plenty to choose from. My job now was to evacuate the wounded and return them to the rear. There were blokes lying around everywhere and the stretcher bearers hurried around picking them up. My carrier was overloaded as I edged away from the battle still raging in the corn field. I even had one bloke laid across the tool box.

This carrier acted up right from the start. It stalled right next to the burnt out carrier with all the wounded Tanki Wallahs on board who had burned to death. With a deal of swearing from all concerned on board I got the carrier going again.

I had not gone far when I ran the carrier into a wadi. The bloke on the tool box disappeared and I thought I had run over him. He soon reappeared and gave me a right mouthful. The carrier refused to start so we abandoned it and the wounded were evacuated on foot.

The battalion pulled out and moved across the front of a battalion from the King's Royal Rifle Corp (KRR). The Germans fired at us as we went, the over-throws killing some KRRs in the process. I now took over a third carrier in the battalion lines, but now the Germans now really had their tails up and they attacked using self-propelled guns. What remained of the battalion's six-pounders drove them off. We withdrew further while still attracting fire from the Germans. My carrier received a very near miss from a large calibre shell but the fragments killed the gunner by the name of Alladyce and another put a hole through the carrier's rad. I had only known the gunner for a few hours.

This carrier now went unserviceable, so I and the commander jumped into another one, my fourth in under a day. We picked up Horace and were ordered to take this carrier to the workshops of the 2nd New Zealand Division some seven miles behind the line – safe from the Germans but alas not the Yanks. While in the New Zealanders' workshops, eighteen Yank Boston medium bombers circled overhead. They decided we were their target, and they unloaded their bombs on the workshops.

After the dust had settled my fourth carrier lay upside down and wrecked and twenty-eight New Zealanders had been killed. One good thing came of this; the three of us stayed as a crew for the rest of the war. The commander, a Welsh Corporal named Morgan, who had won an MM at the 1st Alamein, and the gunner, Horace Kinney, were the only blokes in the battalion at the time who would ride with me. I was considered a bit of a Jonah having lost so many carriers in such a short time which made me a bit of a liability. Morgan had another view. I must be very lucky to still be in one piece, so that was good enough for him and Horace.

While we waited for transport back to battalion, Morgan swanned off to find yet another carrier and Horace and I scrounged a cup of tea. Royal Army Service Corp (RASC) lorries came and went bringing supplies to the New Zealanders. One in particular brought up petrol in the old four-gallon cans which leaked from the seams. His job done, the driver stopped, jumped from his cab and climbed up on to the tail board. Horace and I watched as he disappeared under the canvas tarpaulin, foraged around, and then re-appeared with a primus stove. He placed the stove on the straw which covered the back of the lorry, primed it, and then struck a match. The fumes from the petrol-soaked straw ignited, enveloping the driver in flames. Horace and I ran towards the lorry as the driver panicked and ran back inside it. We waited until he turned and ran to the tailboard, then grabbed him and flung him on to the sand. We began rolling the bloke on the sand to put out the flames but only succeeded in rolling the skin off most of his body and burning my hands. The New Zealander's MO bandaged my hands and told me to report sick but Morgan had, in the meantime, found another carrier and we decided to get back to battalion.

I drove with my hands encased in bandages like boxing gloves while Horace changed gears. Morgan thought we were all round the bend. At battalion I reported to the company commander. He, as was his nature, thought I was swinging the lead and proceeded to remove the bandages. On seeing the state of my hands he ordered me to report to our MO to get them re-bandaged and then to report back for light duties.

These light duties consisted of guarding an upturned Bren carrier with the remains of an officer still inside from last to first light, and to prevent the vehicle and its contents from being looted by the locals. The carrier had turned over on the salt flats after Kournine and caught light. The officer trapped in the commander's position had shot himself. Next morning I was relieved and looked forward to a good kip. Horace however informed me that our carrier, the one knocked out by the Tiger, was in one piece and all our best kit was still intact. There was nothing for it but to sneak off and get our Cairo Gibbets back[1]. (Henry bought these from a full corporal for £5. They were the home service green uniform and were kept for best although it is not known if he ever wore them.)

Morgan came with us as we scrambled through the now abandoned battlefield in front of Kournine. Sure enough there was the carrier which was scorched but still in one piece. Our luck was holding. With no Germans in sight we crept up to one side of it, peered over into the gunner's compartment and came face to face with a couple of Germans going through our kit. Discretion is the greater part of valour, so we backed off and left the German's to their ill-gotten gains.

In the following days and weeks the 1st and 8th Armies attacked the Germans and Italians on both flanks with the aim to join up at Tunis. The 7th Armoured Division was now transferred to the 9th Corps of 1st Army for the assault on Medjez El Bab. Once the attack had succeeded they raced the 6th Armoured Division for the honour of capturing Tunis which eventually fell on 8 May 1943. The war in North Africa was now effectively over.

With the Tunisian campaign over, the battalion moved to Hammam Lif to rest and recuperate. Once the men had cleaned up, leave parties were organized in Tunis. As all the shops had been emptied by the Germans there was little for the men to do so the Army Welfare Service organized an Allied Victory March through the town with the battalion represented by two officers and twenty men.

When the war in North Africa ended, the battalion went into reserve and was not involved in the preparation for the invasion of Sicily. Instead, it was put on standby to return to Britain:

We had a pass to slope off into Tunis from Hammam Lif. Our battalion had been in action for months and it was about time we had a blow from the desert. I had dysentery so had to bolt a lot to the latrine, but this did not stop me from hopping on the three-tonner going into Tunis. In the town we came across a wine bar where the owner tried to overcharge us. So we slung him out and proceeded to drink his stock. We were three sheets to the wind in no time and stumbling out of the bar I realized I wanted to crap. Dysentery gives you no warning so off I ran trying to pull my trousers down at the same time.

I came across what I thought was an empty courtyard so I dropped my trousers and started to do my bits and pieces. It appeared I had gatecrashed the victory parade in Tunis. All of a sudden a staff car pulled up and who should be standing up in the back but Monty himself. I didn't see why

I should stop what I was doing and nor did Monty because he just stood there and saluted me. As the red caps moved in to feel my collar, our own battalion police grabbed me and marched me off with my trousers still around my ankles. They slung me in the back of a lorry going back to our battalion. The Provost Sergeant climbed in the back with me and gave me a right ticking off. I was told to make myself scarce back at battalion, so I lost myself which was a good thing because the red caps turned up and asked to see Bombhead.

He told them in no uncertain terms that it was not one of his riflemen who had relieved himself in front of the army commander. I kept out of Bombhead's way for the rest of the time we were at Hammam Lif!

A series of sports days were also organized. On one particular occasion a bit of desert was cleared for an athletics track. But the engineer's maps did not show the old German minefield on which the track was situated. One bloke was blown up, though he did not receive too serious an injury, and the sports day was abandoned. Some of the blokes were then picked to do 'Bullshit'[2] guards down the Delta while I had the job of driving some of the Allied big noises at the Mena Conference. Winston Churchill and Madam Chiang Kia Shek were particular favourites. The conference took place in late November 1943 and all the delegates, including President Roosevelt, stayed at Mena House.

Madam Chiang Kia Shek was a good-looking bird. She spoke good English and always passed the time of day with the drivers. Winston was a good tipper and sometimes gave his driver a cigar. When I did Bullshit guards for the conference, the section had to sweep the gardens adjacent to the hotel where all the 'big noises' were staying. One morning when we were doing our sweep, there was heavy dew and our KD trousers were soaked through. Winston was on a balcony, saw us and asked what we were doing. We explained we were searching for German paratroopers, to which Winston told us to 'Bugger off' and not to bother. Needless to say we were not asked to do this again.

Any tips would be spent in Cairo at the bars 'owned' by the Rifle Brigade. We drank in the Bystander or sometimes the Mogador. Each regiment had its own bar and fights broke out if members of another regiment chose to cross the threshold. RBs might be invited by the KRRs and vice-versa, but no one else. If a fight did break out a cage would be lowered over the Egyptian band who would sometimes strike up 'God save the King'. All combatants would stand to attention until the last bar was played and then carry on with the fight. Needless to say when the red caps came in, everyone started on them. After a while I got browned off with all this and spent my money with my mates in the NAFFI or YMCA.

The rest of the year was spent away from the frontline as the battalion was held in reserve and the men enjoyed the chance to rest and recover from the intense fighting. But by the following spring they began preparing to leave for Britain as part of the build up for the invasion of Europe. Henry and his friends began to look forward to going home, even if it was only briefly. It would be a chance to see their families and friends again and for Henry a chance to see his girlfriend who had written to him while he was in North Africa. But fate was about to intervene:

We were at last given embarkation orders for our return to Britain to take part in the invasion of northern Europe. All the battalion's vehicles were loaded ready for the move, but at the last minute trouble broke out between factions among the Greek Brigade en route to Italy. A fire fight started in the transit camp and many a bell tent was holed by bullets. After the trouble was sorted out, the Greeks were reorganized and the trouble makers arrested. We, therefore, were earmarked not for home but to take the Greeks' places in Italy. The battalion sailed for Naples in

April 1944. A holiday with pay was our reward and we joined the ranks of the D-Day Dodgers in sunny Italy.

Notes
1. I could not find out what this meant. Lawrence, Henry's son believed 'gibbets' may have been Arabic or Indian slang for clothes. But it may also have been jibbets from jib, the nautical expression used to describe appearance.
2. Bullshit Guard. The battalion picked the smartest soldiers for this guard. In the ranks of the battalion there would be individual soldiers renowned for cleaning boots, squaring off small packs, shining sword scabbards etc. Battledress would be taken to regimental or local tailors to be made to fit perfectly.

Chapter 6

Italy: Operation Diadem

In Italy all the advantages are with the defender. The Germans had constructed a series of defensive lines based on either rivers or mountains. These stretched across Italy and had stopped the Anglo American Armies south of Rome as the winter of 1943 set in. Stalemate now ensued and the armies settled down to conditions like the old Western Front.

The first step in the invasion of Italy had been to capture Sicily in the hope that this would be enough to take Italy out of the war. Already fed up with the conflict, the invasion threw the Italian government into crisis. While Mussolini and Hitler met in northern Italy on 19 July 1943, US warplanes proceeded to bomb Rome. On 25 July King Victor Emanuel had Mussolini arrested and replaced him with Marshall Pietro Badoglio, the Army Chief of Staff who immediately began secret negotiations with the Allies. Thinking Italy would soon be out of the war, plans were made to drop the US 82nd Airborne on Rome. In the meantime Lieutenant General Maxwell D. Taylor negotiated with the new Italian Government and concluded the armistice on 3 September. Italy's surrender was announced on 8 September.

However, the Germans had no intention of surrendering Italy and, belatedly realising it was not going to be an easy conquest, Taylor managed to prevent the paratroops landing in Rome after hastily advising the Allies that they would be cut to pieces by the Germans who had occupied Rome on 10 September. Taylor helped Badoglio form a government in exile in Bari and on 13 October 1943 the Italians declared war on Germany. Some units surrendered to the Germans, while others fought against them and over 500,000 were sent to POW camps from which thousands never returned. The Italian fleet limped into Malta, losing the battleship *Roma* and 1,254 sailors in the process after coming under air attack from their former allies. In Greece 10,000 Italian soldiers died after choosing to fight the Germans. The Germans refused to accept Badoglio as the legitimate Head of State and so they refused to recognise the Italian soldiers as POWs. Thousands were murdered after they surrendered because the Germans chose to classify them as partisans.

In Italy the Germans prepared for the invasion by constructing and strengthening several defensive lines and settled down to fight for every inch of land. They also tried to create a malaria epidemic in the Pontine Marshes south of Rome. The area was strategically important, so in October 1943 the order was given to stop the pumps that drained the marshes. Two German experts on malaria were quickly sent to Italy to advise engineers on how to increase the breeding grounds for this lethal mosquito species. As soon as the Allied advance on Rome was underway the plans were implemented. It had little impact however, as the Allies quickly crossed the Pontine Marshes before the malaria season was underway and then employed massive amounts of DDT to safeguard their supply lines. It was the local population who really suffered when they they returned to their ruined homes and fields after the war, as there was a massive increase in malaria attacks.

Invading Italy from the south was not an easy task. Running down three-quarters of the narrow peninsula were the Apennine Mountains with their steep cliffs, narrow ridges and high jagged peaks which reached over 10,000 feet in places. These towered over narrow valleys. From these mountains there were rivers running down to the sea, all of which crossed the line of the Allied advance. In the places where there were no mountains there were hills and even the flat coastal plains were crisscrossed with rivers, dykes, canals and other water courses. In the Po Valley in the north there was some open country but there they faced the Alps which were even higher than the Apennines. Despite improvements in the rail system the infrastructure was generally poor with few roads linking the isolated villages and small towns. In many of the mountainous areas the only roads were dirt tracks.

Things had begun well. In October 1943 the Allies had taken both Naples and Foggia airfields with little opposition but then the rains had begun swelling the rivers into raging torrents. The retreating Germans had destroyed virtually every bridge and the allied vehicles were soon stuck in roads which had quickly turned into thick glutinous mud.

The civilian population who longed for peace now found themselves caught up in some of the most savage fighting since the First World War. As they retreated northwards, the Germans destroyed crops and burnt villages, and as partisan activity increased so did German reprisals on any villages and towns they thought might have been aiding them. To add to their problems the civilians now faced severe shortages of food. This meant many were on starvation rations as poor infrastructure hampered by Allied bombing meant distribution was intermittent. The problem was exacerbated by increased reprisals, which in turn led to more partisan groups, who in turn needed more food and supplies. Being outside the ration system they had no option but to either rely on the civilian population to feed them or to raid food depots. Because the civilian population was now starving and had little left to give, raids on storage depots increased. This left the authorities with no choice but to store supplies in smaller, more isolated depots, which further exacerbated the existing distribution problems.

The problems were not only on the battleground. The Americans mistrusted British interests in the Mediterranean and had always been reluctant to invade Italy, preferring to concentrate their attack on invading northern France in Operation Overlord. For some reason they had convinced themselves that the British were wavering on Overlord even though there was no proof of this.

The American intention had always been to get together the biggest force possible, invade France and then cross into Germany, defeating them with their superior numbers and technology. After four years of war the British did not have the manpower or resources to commit to a concentrated frontal assault and in any case experience had taught them that it was not always the best way to defeat the Germans. Although they were 100 per cent behind Overlord, they thought it would be better to deplete German manpower and resources first by defeating them elsewhere in North Africa, the Balkans, Russia and Italy.

The Americans also thought Churchill was trying to drag the US into a costly war in the Balkans that would ensure continuing British influence there after the war, although again there was no proof of this. Unlike Roosevelt, Churchill was concerned about Stalin's postwar ambitions. After all, they weren't freeing Europe from Nazi domination to have a Communist regime imposed on it. He therefore considered that the further east Stalin was stopped the better. However the US was not interested. Stalin was an ally and the US had no real post-war ambitions for Europe and intended to leave it to the United Nations to look after. Unfortunately this policy was rather similar to the one they had adopted after the First World War when they had entrusted things to the League of Nations. But as the US was now in the driving seat, the best Britain could hope for were some concessions.

As far as the British were concerned, the Allied invasion of Italy had brought home to them just how difficult it was going to be to liberate France. Therefore, the more German troops that had to remain in Italy the better as this meant there there would be less available in northern France. The invasion had so far ensured that more than fifty German divisions were stuck in Italy and by the end of October there were nearly 400,000 German soldiers there. At the Tehran Conference at the end of November 1943 the British therefore pressed home the need to continue the advance up the toe of Italy.

The Americans finally agreed to postpone Operation Overlord one last time for just a month to give the Allies more time to take Rome and to reach the Pisa (in the east) – Rimini (in the west) Line. But the Americans imposed a strict caveat that from July 1944 a significant amount of men and equipment would be diverted to support the main theatre of war which was the Allied invasion of northern France. This would be done through Operation Anvil, the invasion of southern France. This decision was to have a considerable detrimental impact on the Italian campaign, as from June onwards desperately needed men and equipment would be continually hived off and sent elsewhere. This left the remaining troops with the same objectives, only with fewer men and equipment to achieve them.

The Germans in Italy were led by Field Marshal Albert Kesselring who had begun the war as Commander of 1st Air Fleet which had provided air cover for the invasion of Poland. He had then moved to 2nd Air Fleet where he had supported the invasions of Belgium, Holland and France. He had been made a Field Marshal on 19 July 1940 and, as Commander of the 2nd Air Fleet, had supported the invasion of the Soviet Union. Having been made Commander of all German land and air forces in the Mediterranean, he had stayed in North Africa supporting Rommel after the Luftwaffe had been ordered to concentrate its efforts on the eastern front. On 10 November 1942 he was appointed deputy Commander of Italian forces under Mussolini.

Left to defend against the Allied advance, Kesselring had argued that it would be better to halt the advance south of Rome rather than try and defend the more accessible Pisa–Rimini line further north. He surmised that there were only two realistic routes for the Allies to use to reach Rome from the south. Route 7, or Via Appia, ran along the coast, round the Arunci Mountains and then cut through the Pontine Marshes that were always flooded in the winter. It was very narrow and easily defendable. Route 6 or Via Casilina ran into the Liri Valley. Ten miles south-east of the Liri Valley it passed through the narrow Migano Gap which was ideal for placing artillery. South of the mouth of the Liri River were Monte Cassino and Monte Maio and behind them the mountains. It was here that the Gustav Line ran right across the narrowest point of the peninsula. The Migano Gap and the Gustav Line at Cassino were the most heavily-protected parts of the new defensive system.

Because of the weather only the best roads could be used in the winter and there were few of these. The rivers were swollen which made them difficult to cross, and the low ground of the Liri Valley that lay beneath Monte Cassino had been flooded by the Germans.

Conditions began to resemble the First World War as soldiers crouched in their wet, muddy trenches and dugouts which were subject to almost continual bombardment. Nights were spent making dangerous night-time patrols into no man's land and as the advance stalled, any military gain was often at the expense of far too many casualties. They endured torrential rain and icy winds, ate cold rations and many suffered from trench foot and exposure. They had to haul their own munitions and supplies up and down steep mountainsides as vehicles and even mule trains were often unable to manage the few tracks and rocky crags. Unlike the Germans who could bring equipment and reinforcements by train and road from the north, the Allies were further hampered by having to bring in all their supplies via the sea. They also lacked sufficient manpower to achieve the necessary superiority of at least three to one at the main point of attack. This was vital for the advance to have any chance of success. Even as late as May 1944 the allies only had twenty divisions against Kesselring's twenty-six as all manpower and equipment was now being diverted for the attack on northern Europe.

Until the high ground had been secured, Allied armoured divisions could not pass through the narrow valley along the few roads that could support an armoured advance. But the Germans had placed machine-gun posts and mortar posts in various vantage points that were hidden from view but which afforded them a clear line of fire. Their troops were able to hide amongst rocks and in caves. They could also use the cellars in the houses of the numerous mountain towns and villages as well as the isolated farmhouses. Often they were dug into the reverse side of slopes which protected them from everything apart from the odd mortar round. This made it virtually impossible for the infantry to take the high ground and it meant that a relatively small number of German troops could hold up an entire Allied Division all day:

> An attempt to outflank the Gustav Line with an amphibious operation had led to the landings at Anzio in January 1944. Again stalemate occurred as the Anglo–American force struggled to hang on, let alone break out. Amphibious

operations would out flank the defences but all landing craft had slowly been withdrawn for the invasion of northern Europe. American and British troops had made several attempts to break the deadlock at Monte Cassino from January 1944 with the town and monastery reduced to rubble as first American, French, then Indian and New Zealand and finally British troops tried to break the Gustav Line at Cassino.

When the Anglo-American Armies were re-organized and army lines moved as spring approached, Cassino now came into 8th Army's sector. Plans were put in place for a final break through at Cassino, Operation Diadem, and at Anzio, Operation Buffalo.

By the time Henry arrived in May 1944 a new battle plan had been devised. It had three distinct phases. The first part was to break through and destroy the Gustav Line before Kesselring realised that the amphibious landing threatened further up the coast was just a deception.

The bulk of the British 8th Army (XIII Corps and 2nd Polish Corps) under the command of Lieutenant General Oliver Leese, was moved from the Adriatic front across Italy to join the US 5th Army (US II Corps and French Expeditionary Corps). Here they would attack along a twenty-mile mile front between Cassino and the sea. The US II Corps on the left would attack along the line of Route 7 towards Rome while the French Corp to the right would use the bridgehead across the Garigliano into the Aurunci Mountains – the barrier between the coastal plain and the Liri Valley. This bridge-head had been originally created by X Corps back in January during the first battle. In the centre right the British XIII Corps would attack along the Liri Valley and on the right the Polish Corps (3rd and 5th Division) would attempt to isolate the monastery and push round behind it into the Liri Valley where they would link up with XIII Corps. This pincer movement was the key to the overall success. The Canadian 1st Corps would be held in reserve and once the German 10th Army had been defeated, the US VI Corps would push out of Anzio to cut off the retreating Germans in the Alban Hills.

Because it was intended to be a surprise attack, troop movements had to be carried out in small units. This took two months to achieve. Dummy road signs and radio traffic were created and the US 36th Division did amphibious assault training to give the impression that a sea-borne invasion was being planned north of Rome. Troop movements were confined to darkness and armoured units moving from the Adriatic left behind dummy tanks so any ariel reconnaissance would see no change to the area. This was to ensure Kesselring kept his reserves back from the Gustav Line. The deception was extremely successful as, even by late on the second day of the battle, Kesselring still thought the Allies only had six divisions facing his four on the Cassino front, when in fact they had thirteen.

In the next phase the Allies had to break the second line of defence known by the Allies as the Hitler Line. The Germans had originally named it the Fuhrer Line but were ordered by Hitler to rename it after he realised that if it was overrun this could have an adverse psychological effect. Although the Germans had renamed it the Senger Line after General von Senger und Etterlin, one of the generals commanding Axis forces in the area, the Allies continued to refer to it as the Hitler line.

The third phase of the battle would see the now reinforced US led VI Corps break out from the Anzio bridgehead and cut off the retreating German army. The date for the launch of the battle was originally set for April but was then moved back to May. This was to allow the weather to improve sufficiently so that the Allies' heavily-armoured superiority could be used to best advantage. It would also give them time to build up the desired three-to-one manpower superiority and for the troops who had been fighting all through the winter to be rested, refitted and reinforced. From the middle of March, allied Air Forces began carrying out Operation Strangle. Roads, railway lines and bridges were subject to continual bombing from Cassino to 150 miles north of Rome in a concentrated attempt to destroy all German supply and communication lines:

> Our battalion disembarked at Naples, got ourselves organized and then went into the line near Cassino in May 1944;

61st Infantry Brigade had come into being at the end of May. It had been intended to bring over another British Armoured Division from Tunisia but the roads in Italy were not suitable, so only one British Armoured Division, the 6th, could be used. With the 2nd and 10th Battalions of the Rifle Brigade now in Italy, 8th Army decided to tidy things up and convert us and the 2nd into Lorried infantry, keep the 10th as the motor battalion and group us all into 61st Infantry Brigade. We would come under the command of 6th Armoured Divsion and with 1st Guards Infantry Brigade, 8th Army would have a very powerful formation in its order of battle. A commanding officer for the brigade was needed. One had actually been chosen but he was still fighting with his Brigade at Anzio. Brigadier Adrian Gore was a rifleman, and he had commanded 10RB in Tunisia.

Henry arrived in Naples in early May 1944, the battalion having set sail from Alexandria in two convoys. The sun was shining, the water a shimmering blue which reflected the cloudless sky, and after the dust and dirt of the desert, Naples seemed like a pleasant change. Unlike those who had arrived earlier in the year, Henry had little time to see the darker, seedier side, the filthy streets, the all-encompassing poverty, crime and prostitution that characterised the sea port of a country that was being torn apart by a war most of its people were heartily sick of. The men passed quickly through the town and headed for their allotted assembly area in the wooded countryside around Villa Volturno near Capua. Their orders were to be ready for battle by 28 May.

Chapter 7

Dust is Death

On May 11 at 23.00, the fourth battle of Cassino began with a massive artillery bombardment from 1,000 guns on the 8th Army front and 600 on the 5th Army front. Although the biggest contingent were British and US troops, there were also French, Poles, Moroccans, Algerians, Canadians, New Zealanders (including Maoris) and South Africans (white, black, Asian and Zulus). There were also several Australians and Rhodesians in the Air Force.

An hour and a half later and all four sectors were engaged in battle. Although by daylight the US II Corps had made little progress, the French Corps had quickly achieved their objectives and were fanning out towards the 8th Army on their right. XIII Corps (British 4th Infantry Division and 8th Indian Division) had crossed the Rapido despite strong opposition and in the mountains above Cassino the Polish infantry fought tenaciously for three days against determined opposition in conditions that resembled 'a miniature Verdun'[1].

By the afternoon of 12 May the Rapido bridgeheads were increasing, but the war of attrition in the mountains was continuing. Finally, by 13 May, the Germans began to give way to the 5th Army. This was despite being reinforced by reserves in an attempt to give the others time to withdraw to Kesselring's preferred line of defence, the Senger Line which was some eight miles to the rear. The French had now captured Monte Maio so could assist on the right of the 5th Army, and the Moroccan Goumiers[2] had outflanked the German defence by using the mountains parallel to the Liri Valley. These were undefended as the Germans had considered them to be impassable.

On 15 May the British 78th Division was bought up from reserve to help isolate Cassino from the Liri Valley and on 17 May the Polish Corps renewed its assault on Cassino. By 18 May they had linked up two miles west of Cassino. Early on 18 May a Polish reconnaissance group, the 12th Podolian Uhlan Regiment, found the monastery abandoned. The Germans had withdrawn overnight to take up their new defensive positions on the Senger Line. The only Germans they found were a group of pale, worn out, emaciated soldiers who were too sick to be moved.

As the 8th Army advanced slowly up the Liri Valley the 5th Army continued its advance up the coast. The immediate follow up assault by the 8th Army had failed so they paused and regrouped. The next assault began on 23 May with the Polish Corps attacking Piedimonte on the right while the 1st Canadian Infantry Division attacked in the centre. By 24 May the Canadians had breached the line, allowing the 5th Canadian Armoured Division to pour through the gap. By 25 May Piedimonte had fallen and the way to Rome was clear:

> After hard fighting in early May, both operations achieved success and the German Armies were in a situation where they would be destroyed south of Rome. Brigadier Gore joined and the pursuit from the Gustav Line began.

At 04.00 on the morning of 29 May the Brigade moved off from the Villa Volturno and by dawn had made good progress down Route 6, the highway between Naples and Rome which passed through Cassino. But after a while they found the road was heavily mined so they had no option but to make the rest of the way along narrow tracks and through thick dust clouds that swirled around them, clogging their throats and lungs and making them cough. Every so often they passed signs warning that 'Dust is Death – Watch your Dust' as the enemy would regularly shell dust clouds. They didn't really need the warnings as the dust was already becoming a serious problem even though they were only travelling at about five miles per hour instead of the official eight.

The main problem was that the gap between the tarpaulin and the tailboard seemed to act like a vacuum cleaner and sucked the dust into the truck. Frustrated they tried letting down the flap of the tarpaulin but within minutes there was a complete lack of air which meant they had no option but to open it again. They even tried taking it off, no easy job while the truck was still moving. But that was even worse as it just exposed them to the glare from the sun which bounced off the steel girders on the truck. Together with the dust which seemed to shimmer bright white in the sunlight, the glare blinded them. Eventually they replaced the tarpaulin and tried to ignore the dust as it poured in, even though at times it was so thick they couldn't see their friends across the other side of the truck. It wasn't just inside the dust was a problem as outside it reduced visibility to inches and slowed their progress even more. By midday the sun was high in a cloudless blue sky and the temperature had risen even more. The thick dust continued to choke them and the men slumped in their seats feeling completely exhausted. Even the atheists among them prayed that it wouldn't be long before they stopped. Fortunately they didn't have too much longer to suffer, as by the early afternoon they found themselves back on a main road where they stopped for a quick brew up and were able to eat their bully and biscuits.

Feeling much better they climbed back aboard the crowded truck and in the late afternoon they approached the outskirts of Cassino. Although it had been cleared of enemy troops ten days earlier, they never really saw the main town as it was so full of rubble that the road through the middle was still only operating as a one-way street. As they came within two miles of the town they were diverted through the outskirts. Everywhere they looked there were piles of rubble, and the air was filled with the sickly distinctive smell of decomposing bodies that were still buried underneath the wrecked buildings. Burnt-out carriers and tanks littered the side of the roads with more swollen corpses rapidly decomposing in the stifling heat and covered in flies and maggots. As much as they had hated the dust they were glad to get back out into the countryside and the relatively cooler air. Conversation was muted and many dozed or closed their eyes and tried not to think about the things they'd seen.

As night fell the temperature began to drop and they pulled up at the side of the road. After a while a despatch rider arrived with some vacuum flasks containing stew, rice pudding and tea. Relieved to be off the trucks and in cooler air the mood improved and after finishing their meal they settled down for the night. They moved off again at dawn and now found themselves on an extremely bumpy diversion off the road and through some half-filled mine craters which caused the truck to buck and rear all over the place. Henry began to long for the time they would arrive at wherever they were going and could finally dismount from the trucks. In the meantime they did at least have some of the propaganda leaflets the retreating Germans had left behind. The latest one was all about American GIs attacking Italian women and was so ludicrous that it at least gave them something to laugh at.

Despite these delays, by the early afternoon the brigade had reached their new assembly point just beyond Aquino and had passed into the command of 6th British Armoured Division. Their first task was to secure the perimeter against any attempted German infiltration into the main axis of XIII Corps' advance. This they did by placing a series of piquet[3] anti tank weapons on the hills east of Arce. Then they settled down to wait for the order to advance.

On 2 June the Brigade was ordered to move to a new concentration area fifteen miles further along Route 6. Moving north towards Rome, Henry caught glimpses of the gentle rolling countryside that bordered the road. The Germans had retreated so quickly here that they had not too much time to destroy the crops and buildings in their path. The weather was hot and sunny and everywhere he looked there were fields of cypresses and vines, the fruits ripening in the hot sun. However, the dust was just as bad as it had been earlier. Lack of rain meant that even the main highway was now covered in choking clouds of grit which swirled round them creating even more visibility problems and caking everything in a thick white layer of dust. Despite this the convoy slowly advanced towards the next objective. But it still took considerably longer than expected as priority on all the main routes was being given to the 78th Division, all Canadian traffic and in fact everyone, it seemed, except them. As they crawled slowly forward they suddenly found themselves in action for the first time in nearly a year as they faced some light opposition from a rearguard of scattered infantry and a few guns. This resistance was soon overcome and their reward was the capture of four guns and forty prisoners. Slowly, relentlessly, they pressed on and eventually reached their harbour area in woods west of the road that was south of Alatri. It was here they settled down for the night.

Henry stretched out on his bed roll and looked up at the cloudless night sky above him. The sky here seemed much smaller than it did in the desert with the stars that much further away. It felt good to be among trees again though after the vast emptiness of the desert and he found the gentle breeze rustling the leaves above him soothing and reminiscent of home. Thinking of home made him think back over the images he had seen in the past few days and his shock at the amount of destruction they had passed through. Many towns and villages had been reduced to nothing more than piles of rubble. How anyone could have survived in those conditions he had no idea. The people they had passed had looked pale, emaciated and worn out. Many were injured or had missing limbs. Even those who had been delighted to see them wore the haunted expressions of those who had seen too much. Henry turned over and closed his eyes. Now was not the time for too much thinking. It was time to rest and get ready for the next battle. Judging by what he had seen and what he had heard from others, he was going to need all his strength to survive the next few weeks or months. Within minutes he was in a deep sleep; the world forgotten for a few precious hours.

As the Brigade pushed forward events around them moved on. The Germans now declared Rome an open city and withdrew. The German 10th Army retreating from the Gustav Line found itself caught between the US and Canadian Forces. It seemed the perfect opportunity to cut them off and destroy them. American General Mark Clark was given orders to do this but instead decided to send his US Forces towards Rome. On June 4 1944 he entered the undefended city of Rome and the German 10th Army escaped. Two days later General Alexander was ordered to push north as quickly as possible to try and prevent the Germans digging in. The 5th Army now set out to capture the port of Civitavecchia, the airfields at Viterbo and the Pisa–Lucca–Pistoia triangle on the Arno River, while the 8th Army targeted the Florence–Arezzo–Bibbiena triangle.

To maintain speed they were ordered to bypass any enemy strong-holds but at the same time exploit any opportunity to split or destroy the German X and XIV armies before they reached Arno.

Because of the constant replacement of troops who had been withdrawn for Operation Anvil neither the 5th nor the 8th Army were able to move forward as quickly as intended although Civitavecchia and Viterbo did fall to the 5th Army on 7 June and the 8th Army captured Terni and Perugia on the 13 June and 19 June respectively. They also encountered further delays caused by the difficult terrain they had to traverse, numerous demolitions, booby traps and mined roads, some unexpected bad weather and logistical problems. There were also pockets of sporadic, but often stiff, resistance from small numbers of German forces who were determined to hold up the Allied advance for as long as possible to allow the main armies to retreat:

> We were dismounted again; 6th Armoured was taking up a lot of road so our battalion and the second (2RB) were converted to lorried infantry. This didn't mean the carriers were not used, so 10RB and the Guards kept their motor platoons. Good job I was out of the carriers on this occasion. I was back in 3 platoon and we were waiting on the side of the road as three carriers from the Guards came through us. All the riflemen were undercover in the verges; the engineers had done their job and cleared all the nasty surprises. Three Guards' carriers came past and there was no one to our front as the Germans had cleared off. We were creeping slowly up the Arno Valley towards Perugia I think it was. The first Dripping's[4] carrier moved forward; the second about 100 yards behind, and the last the same again as back stop. We watched to see what happened and sure enough the Germans did have a surprise.
>
> The second carrier suddenly hit a mine. There was this flash followed by a bang and the front of the carrier disappeared. The commander, who had been standing up, was blown out of the vehicle by the blast. He went quite a few feet up in the air and then, like a puppet with all its strings

broken, crashed back down to earth. Everyone was stunned and someone said, 'Cor did you see that?' Another said 'Glad that weren't me'. We watched as the first Guards carrier tried to reverse back up the road keeping clear of their bloke and the carrier which was now alight. A couple of our stretcher bearers shot off up the road, and soon returned with the commander on a stretcher. We asked 'Well?' The stretcher bearers shook their heads and one said: 'Every bone is his body is broke by the looks of it'. We could see this as his legs had been blown up into his chest. The stretcher bearers confirmed that the 'rest of the crew are dead too.' No one was surprised and everyone did a bit in their trousers as they realised what the invasion of Italy was going to be like.

The next German defences were the Senger Line; 6th Armoured Division had attacked and after heavy fighting had broken through into the Arno Valley. One action we fought was against a rearguard of German mountain troops and a couple of 88mm anti-aircraft guns. As the tanks approached, the Germans fired a Spandau and the whole division stopped. The Tanki Wallahs were of the opinion that if there was a Spandau, then 88s must be in the vicinity. They were correct, but the Germans, fearing they would not be able to get the guns away, had blown their barrels.

'A' company were in support of the tanks. I was in number 3 platoon made up mainly of the men from the company's scout platoon. We dismounted from the lorry and began working around behind the Germans. For a while we came under some intense machine-gun fire and you could see the tops of the corn being cut away as the gun fired at ankle height. The platoon officer kept shouting for us to keep going, but me and another bloke jumped into a trench which turned out to be a German latrine. The bottom of the trench was still better than a Spandau. The noise a Spandau makes is the one thing I will always remember. It sends shivers down the spine and will cut you in half. We lost an officer from another platoon that day when he was blown in two. We waited a while until we could not stand the smell anymore and then scrambled out. Fixing swords, we crept up to the German position and gained complete surprise. They had no stomach for a fight and surrendered at once. We marched our haul of thirty-five prisoners to the rear past the tanks. The riflemen exchanged a healthy banter with their crews and did very little to hide their opinion of them either.

These prisoners did not know how lucky they were. Our only loss this day was an officer, a popular man within company. However, our treatment of these prisoners was observed by their comrades further along the road. We made sure they were given a fag each but also made sure they were between us and their mates. Over the next few days the Germans would wait on the side of the road to give themselves up to any British troops who came along. There are many ways to undermine the enemy and taking prisoners is one of them.

The battalion halted for three days north of Rome at a place called Tivoli. The city had been taken by the American 5th Army and thus most of the German Armies were allowed to escape.

After a short break they were on the move again. Their job now was to secure the hills on either side of the road towards Perugia. The advance was agonisingly slow as they cautiously picked their way through the cultivated vines and olive groves, ever alert for the slightest movement that would indicate an enemy presence. The sun beat down from a cloudless sky and the air was intensely hot, still and humid as they slowly made their way through the closely-planted trees. Every step was fraught with danger as the heavy cultivation offered numerous opportunities for snipers and the thick lush undergrowth provided excellent hiding places for mines:

Our next actions were against rearguards of mixed units. We progressed up the Arno River Valley towards Perugia; the riflemen securing the hills either side of the road which allowed the tanks to edge forward. Every now and again we would come up against a demolished bridge. Usually the approaches were mined and a strong German rear-guard dug in. Casualties began to mount, not many at a time, but still enough over a week to wear down a platoon. When we did reach an Italian village, the platoons would go straight through and dig in facing the Germans. Counter-attacks from the Germans were common; sometimes they might not even let you leave the village before they would mortar the place. During one particular action we caught German rearguards before they could get away. A couple of platoons went in, one jumping over the back garden walls, the other waiting for the Germans as they tried to escape. One of our blokes said that they were only separated by the wall from the Germans on a couple of occasions. Italian civilians caught up in the action risked their lives standing at the windows pointing at the Germans waiting for our blokes to move. They were sorted out with a hand grenade.

On another occasion further north the villagers were on the streets as we arrived; only women and children, as most of the men had bolted up into the hills. I followed a Sherman in the carrier and the locals began clapping. They had nothing to give us as the Germans had taken everything. One woman had her child in hand and as the Sherman drew level with her, the kid suddenly ran and went straight under the tank's tracks.

Near Perugia we pulled off the road beside an olive grove. Our battalion was now fifty odd miles in front of the rest of 61st Infantry Brigade. It began to rain so the tanks pulled off the road and the crews made themselves comfort-able for the night under their tanks. It poured during the night and the ground became waterlogged. Soon the tanks started to sink, pinning the crews under them. It was a right old balls up, what with the Tanki Wallahs all crushed under their tanks. We tried digging them out but in the end there was nothing for it but to pull the tanks on to drier ground.

You can imagine the state the blokes were in when they pulled tanks off the top of them.

The Luftwaffe still flew sorties so air attacks were not uncommon. On this particular occasion a Thunderbolt appeared from the direction of the German lines. It was not unusual to see an allied aircraft coming back so no one took any notice as he did a victory role over a RASC column further down the road. He circled back, picked up speed in a dive then opened fire at the middle of the column. Lorries exploded or swung from the road as the Thunderbolt flew low past us in the olive grove. We saw the black crosses on the fuselage and the pilot sticking two fingers up at us as he roared away.

The battalion now went into reserve and we got down to some maintenance on our vehicles as mechanised warfare is hard on both men and equipment. We were always ready for a quick move though and sure enough Bombhead decided to move at 0630 next morning. He always had a bit of theatre about him, so at 0625 out came his hunting horn on which he played the battalion call for move. His battalion replied with a series of impressions of yapping dogs. The officers did not know what to do and some suppressed a smile. The upshot was that Bombhead never blew his horn again.

By 21 June the Germans had retreated 110 miles north of Rome with the Allies in hot pursuit. But the advancing Allies were not the only problem the Germans were facing. Partisan activity had also increased considerably after the fall of Rome, and German supplies, equipment and soldiers were coming under continued attack. The Germans initially retaliated by taking hostages from the local civilian population and setting fire to the farmhouses in their area. But this failed to stop partisan activity, if anything it grew steadily worse. Eventually the problem became so bad that Kesselring decided to allow his commanders carte blanche on how they dealt with it in their respective areas. This led to the beginning of several horrific massacres of the civilian population. In Niccioleta in West

Tuscany eighty-three men were executed on 13 June. In Gubbio on 21 June forty men were executed and on the 23–24 June more than thirty men, women and children were murdered in the tiny village of Bettola in Emilia Romagna. On 29 June the Fallschirm Panzerkorps of Herman Goering massacred 212 people including women, children and babies. The Germans made no effort to hide the massacres as the whole point was for them to act as a warning for the partisans and other civilians. Several times advancing troops came across the results of these massacres and where they could, would bury those they found. But it was not just the unburied remains of civilians that littered the villages and countryside. The bodies of those who died in the battles between the retreating Germans and advancing Allies often lay where they had fallen as there was not always time to bury them. Their swollen corpses added to the increasing horror of the Italian Campaign; a campaign in which civilians were to suffer as much as the men who were fighting.

Notes
1. Col Heilmann of the 4th Parachute Regiment.
2. In 1943 the Goumiers who were colonial troops were formed into four Groups of Moroccan Tabors (GTM), each consisting of three loosely organized Tabors (roughly equivalent to a battalion) who specialised in mountain warfare.
3. This was an improvised AT mine which used a 3.5kg explosive charge and a 120mm artillery shell dug vertically in the ground. It had a one metre-long stake attached to the rupture igniter.
4. Dripping and Lards ... Cockney rhyming slang for Guards.

Chapter 8

Dig or Die

The next objective for the battalion was Perugia, part of the Albert Line which ran from Ancona on the Adriatic coast to the Tyrrhenian coast opposite the island of Elba. The fighting would be concentrated on a line between the walled town of Chiusi, through Santacchio, to the south-west corner of Lake Trasimeno. The line west of Lake Trasimene was known by the British as the Trasimene Line and consisted of a series of hastily prepared defensive positions that were five miles wide and fifteen miles deep.

The rolling countryside between the lake and the mountains was known as the Chiana Valley and was previously a swamp that had been drained in the fifteenth century. Now it was home to numerous olive groves, small fields of grain and vineyards, and isolated farmhouses. The Germans had transformed these sturdily-built farmhouses into miniature fortresses while their engineers had used mines and other explosive devices to turn the small drainage ditches and stream beds into anti-tank barriers. Apart from Highway 71, which ran alongside the lake, all the other roads were little more than tracks that became thick with mud and virtually impassable after just three days of rain and continued vehicle movement.

The German X Army had ordered its three best divisions, the Herman Goering Panzer Division, 1st Paratroop Division and 334th Infantry Division, to defend this sector. Despite this, the Germans realised that it was unlikely they would be successful, unless extra resources were found to stop the 5th Army's rapid advance along the coast:

The city of Perugia is situated near Lake Trasimeno and formed part of the next German defensive, the Albert Line. It was 61st Infantry Brigade's task to take the heights north-east of Perugia which would effectively cut Route 71 and bring the lake under observation. This action became known to history as the Battle of Trasimeno. Lasting from 20 June to 28 June the fighting was every bit as hard as Cassino with the Germans holding on for grim death.

General Sidney Kirkman who was commanding XIII Corps had decided to mount a co-ordinated attack on the Trasimene Line using the 6th South African Armoured Division, 4th Infantry Division and 78th Division. The battle began at the villages of Sanfatuccio and Puccianelli. Behind Sanfatuccio there was a church which was situated on higher ground. The Germans had fortified the church and were using the high ground on which it stood to give them the advantage over their attackers. As the 75mm guns began blasting the houses at close range, the riflemen swiftly followed and stormed the buildings. Intense house-to-house fighting ensued with mounting casualties on both sides as the Germans fought tenaciously to hold each position. The civilian population who had remained in the villages cowered in their cellars praying for survival as the battle raged above and around them, reducing their homes to little more than piles of rubble.

Meanwhile, at 1700 hrs on 19 June, Lieutenant Colonel Douglas Darling DSO MC, received orders that 7RB were to capture Monte Malbe that night. Monte Malbe was not particularly steep and had no distinct summit but it was 654 metres high. Other than a small red-roofed farmhouse near the summit and two rows of trees behind this on the north side, the terrain was bare rock. This would make it extremely hard to assault as there was little cover. The defenders would definitely have the advantage as from the top there was an excellent view of Perugia to the east, Lake Trasimene to the west and the roads to the south. However, it did not completely command the high ground to the north as it was overshadowed by Monte Tezio which was 961 metres high and this was the real dominating feature. The ground in the dip in between these two

Henry before the battle of El-Alamein.

Henry at the end of the Tunisian champagne.

Lt.Col. Douglas Darling (centre) 'Bombhead', Italy 1945.

Officers of 61st Infantry Brigade and 26th Armoured Brigade, Italy 1945.

7RB's advance along the Italian peninsular, 1944-45.

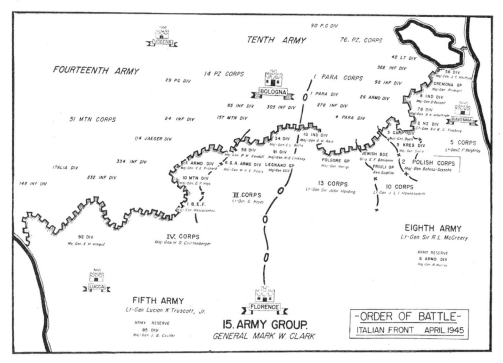

Operation 'Grapeshot', 15th Army Groups final offensive in Italy, April 1945.

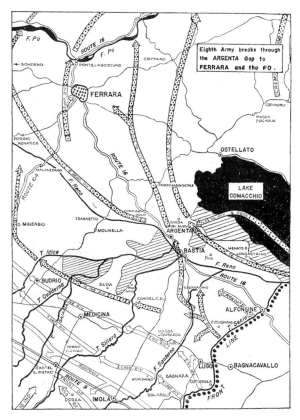

Operation 'Buckland', 8th Army's offensive through the Argenta Gap, April/May 1945.

Henry, in Austria, at the end of the war, 1945.

Henry on holiday in Cornwall.

General Mark Clark (GOC 15th Army Group) and Gen. Sir Richard McCreery (GOC 8th Army) inspect guard of honour from 7RB.

Henry and Dorothy on their wedding day.

Henry's call up paper for the Korean War.

Trassamino Line: Advance on Perugia. Railway station, today, from which 7RB approached. (Monte Malbe in the background)

Trassamino Line: Advance on Perugia. Forestry Hut, today, containing German OP captured by A Coy 7RB.

Trassamino Line: Advance on Perugia. Church at Corciano, occupied by 10RB.

Tossignano today.

Borgo Tossignano today.

Centre of Tossignano today.

Henry and Dorothy in the square at Poggio Renatico.

hills was very broken and thickly wooded in places, making it extremely difficult to secure. But despite these limitations it was still considered to be a very necessary objective.

As 10 RB already held Monte Lacugnano, from which most of the surrounding terrain could be seen, they were ordered to recce the area. Once this was complete an outline plan for the assault was made. It was now after dark even though it was mid-summer and further time was needed to disseminate the orders down to the platoons and section commanders and to get the men sorted out and rested if necessary. Thus it was several hours later, at 01.00 hours, when they finally set out. The plan was to capture the objective while it was still dark but not to give the enemy the opportunity to counter-attack until daylight.

It was a very dark night and raining heavily. The men set off on a five-mile march to L'Olmo which was the junction of the track up into the mountains:

> Our battalion's objective was a feature known as Monte Malbe. It had to be taken and held at all costs. Before we moved, Bombhead did a recce of the area and the approaches over which we could conduct a night march; 15th Panzer grenadier division were identified from captured prisoners. The battalion were brought forward by lorry, we dismounted, and following a narrow gauge rail line we began our night march of five miles. This gave the 'Teds'[1], as we called them by now, no prior warning of our approach and our forward platoon captured the garrison of the railway station at the bottom of Malbe asleep.
>
> We now pushed two companies up the hill, left one halfway down and anchored the whole thing with another company holding a huddle of farm buildings on the flat. German counter-attacks, when they came in, would be along the shoulders of the hill thus cutting off the forward companies. This is why we left one company halfway up. Our progress up the hill was hindered by the agricultural terraces – which are a regular feature in Italy – and the now sporadic mortar fire coming in from the Germans.

The speed at which the Germans reacted was always fast, and soon dead and wounded men from the forward platoons began tumbling back down the terraces. Speed would be the essence of this attack and in the end all that mattered was who reached the top first. We were determined it would be us. A track was found on which the Germans were trying to haul up a large calibre gun using oxen. One of the beasts was dispatched with a rifle shot and the gun and crew were captured. Our forward platoons cracked on and reached the top of Malbe capturing some more Germans on the summit.

We began trying to dig in. The soil in this part of Italy is very thin and rock is found just under the surface. Not only does this produce showers of splinters when a shell lands, it means a slit trench is not deep enough. The best bet was to use Sangers and we had just finished ours when the first German counter-attack came in at first light. Taking careful aim as the Germans came over the top of the hill; the riflemen took a toll of the attackers which caused the Germans to change tactics.

In the middle of the position was a small, red, Italian Forestry hut. The Germans had used it as an OP (Observation Post) and we pressed it into service as a company HQ with a link back to the artillery at the bottom of our side of the hill. The fire from our guns proved crucial. They fired at a high trajectory landing shells just over the brow of the hill directly on the German attacks as they developed. However 'Ted' was a good soldier and he started his infiltration tactics using a line of poplar trees opposite the red hut, and, as we suspected, the shoulders of the hill. The company at the bottom of the hill came under small arms fire, and snipers were left behind when the counter-attacks withdrew. The 10th battalion were also hanging on grimly to their gains, giving as good as it got.

Soon the red hut was coming under direct small arms fire. The company radio operator on his own initiative radioed the artillery to shorten the range and thus brought fire directly down on the area in front of the hut. This stopped the Germans cold. Soon the forward companies were receiving fire from all directions. The company half way up the hill started losing men to snipers and all the time shell (ours and the Germans') landed on the hill. I now realised the predicament I was in.

I was the Bren gunner in an infantry platoon and my section was holding a flank. We had five blokes try to bolt as we were coming up the terraces. A burst from my Bren stopped them but as the counter-attacks began they scarpered, leaving me and another bloke to hold a section front of about one hundred yards.

This did not improve my mood as I had fallen down one of the old Roman grave pits on the approach march which dot the land around Trasimeno, losing a lot of bark from my arms and legs. These pits dated from the Punic Wars between Carthage and Rome. The battle between these two giants of antiquity around Trasimeno led to the name The Plain of Blood being used for the flat land around the lake. Anyway back to 1944. Our platoon sergeant came round and discovered our predicament and with the promise of reinforcements he doubled off to find the officer.

To maintain the radio link between the companies, a radio Bren-carrier was stationed halfway up the track. The battalion was consolidating its position and the Germans were becoming more desperate. To increase our firepower on the hill, Bombhead managed to get a Sherman (17/21st Lancers) up the track and positioned to fire at the Germans in support of both us and 10RB.

Most of the German effort had now switched to evicting a company from 10RB who occupied the village on their side of Malbe. German snipers were still active as were their mortars, so I was detailed off to support the radio-carrier down the track. Leaving the Bren with another bloke, I picked up a rifle and trotted off down the track. Standing talking to the radio operator I felt the draught of a bullet pass my shoulder and a neat hole appeared in the bloke's head. This was either one hell of a shot, or the Ted had aimed at me and missed. I did not wait around and doubled around the other side of the carrier.

Things were still nip and tuck. We later heard that 10RB had lost a whole company on the hill next to Malbe, so to keep our heads down Ted increased the harassing fire on us. It was now 22 June, so we'd had little sleep for thirty-six hours, and to make things worse Bombhead became a casualty to shell splinters. He came past me at the radio-carrier not long after the operator had been shot. He was supported by an officer and was as white as a sheet.

Although the Germans had constructed two further defensive lines, the Dora and Trasimeno (Frieda) Lines, the Allied advance had overrun both these lines by the end of June:

On 28 June the Germans withdrew. Their losses were substantial in men and equipment. They had hoped to turn the Albert Line into another Gustav Line. Elements of several German divisions joined battle with us in and around Perugia; 1st Guards took Perugia and 6th Armoured Division played a big part in battle. German military intelligence had failed to identify two further Rifle Brigade battalions in Italy until we lost a prisoner at Malbe. From then on for the next few months we met paratroopers.

Kesselring's strategy of fall back, stand, fight; fall back, stand, fight, as the Germans steadily withdrew back to the Gothic Line, was successfully delaying the Allied advance. This would give the Germans valuable time to reinforce the Gothic Line, the last major defence line in Italy, and make the Allies' task that much harder. Furthermore it would allow the weather to play its part as first the autumn rains and then the winter snow bought the Allied advance to a virtual standstill.

Note

1. This was a shortened version of Tedeschi, the Italian for Germans.

Chapter 9

There is No Such Thing as an Atheist if You are Being Shelled

By 5 July XIII Corps was pressing north to the Arezzo Line. This was the last serious defensive line south of Florence and was a narrow valley held by a small detachment of the German X Army group:

> The next large town was Arezzo and our battalion kept up the pressure; still climbing up hills to secure the summits before the tanks moved forward. On one of these hills, Monte Maggio, 'A' company fought a very stiff action against German Paratroopers who proved a different kettle of fish from the other Germans we had met.

For Henry and the other men of 7RB, July had started with a three-day break in what seemed like the hottest days of the summer so far. The sun blazed down from a cloudless blue sky bathing the countryside in a hazy glow of stifling heat. The men gratefully took the rare opportunity to relax and to catch up on letter writing, washing, sleeping and generally resting. As with all holidays the first day seemed to stretch out endlessly as they basked in the hot mid-summer sun. There were few houses where they were and even less shade and, as the southern shore of Lake Trasimene was full of reeds and rather slimy mud, it made swimming rather unattractive for all but the most determined.

The nights were warm and balmy, the sky clear and filled with stars. The full moon bathed everything in a bright glow and evenings were spent at one of the open-air cinema shows or lying quietly reading, playing cards and generally relaxing. Henry spent his time writing to his girlfriend and his parents, although it was increasingly difficult to think of what to write. Most of the things he was witnessing he could not write about and because of censorship he also had to be careful he didn't inadvertently say anything that could describe the battalion's position. This meant writing letters took considerably longer than normal.

On the other hand no one really seemed interested in them now. Most of the letters they received just talked about northern Europe and the fighting that was taking place there. It seemed that Italy was never mentioned in the press or on the radio, giving the impression that very little was happening in Italy and that the real action and the real heroes were in France.

Their plight had been made worse by the insensitive remarks of Lady Astor, MP for Plymouth, who commented along the lines that there were lots of troops in Italy doing nothing, but happy to stay there and so avoid the fighting in Normandy. Given the enormous number of casualties, the extremely difficult fighting conditions and the very determined resistance they were facing, most of them felt very hurt and offended by the apparent trivialisation of their campaign. In true cynical 8th Army style they now had several versions of a song called 'We're the D-Day Dodgers' written by Major Hamish Henderson of the 51st Highland Division to the tune of 'Lili Marlene' which they sang quite often. But it didn't stop the real anger and frustration they felt. If only the Germans felt the same about Italy as they did at home the campaign would soon be over and we'd be on our way back Henry thought wryly as he struggled to find something to write about.

They heard little from the enemy during those three days other than a couple of Luftwaffe raids on one night when they dropped some butterfly bombs on the camp. There was little damage and no injuries but it did interrupt one of the open air cinema films.

Lieutenant Colonel Dick Fyffe MC had now taken control of 7RB, and as enemy resistance appeared to be weakening and the only fighting was against rearguards covering the withdrawal, it was assumed there would be no serious resistance until they reached the Gothic Line. But yet again they had seriously underestimated the enemy's determination. The next objective, which had been identified as being Pontassieve, took nearly two months to take.

The divisional axis Route 71 ran along the edge of the Chiana Valley to Arezzo. The valley itself was thickly cultivated with vines and orchards and crisscrossed by dykes and irrigation channels. It was bordered on the left by a canal and on the right by mountains, and the road itself ran alongside the foot of the mountains.

The advance along Route 71 towards Arezzo began on 4 July. After the stifling heat of the first few days of July it had now begun to rain heavily. This made cross-country movement difficult, leaving the division strung out along the highway at the mercy of the enemy who were overlooking them on the high ground to the right. There were anti-tank guns in front which prevented them from moving forward and they couldn't work round to the left because of the canal. Before long it became evident that the high ground on the right of the highway would have to be cleared. If not, the leading troops would be vulnerable to continued firing, shelling and mortaring from the guns that were well positioned in the observation posts on the hill.

The 7th Battalion was given the task of clearing the high ground. There were three features that needed to be cleared; Monte Castiglion Maggio which stood a few miles south of Arezzo, Monte Lignano which was four miles to the north, and Monte Camurcino which was more remote but also overlooked the road. The most important part of the clearing operation would be the attack on Monte Castiglion Maggio. The mountain was partially covered in scrub and trees and had no clearly defined summit which made it very complicated to take:

> Monte Maggio is near Arezzo and we had a right barrow full with these German paratroopers. Two companies did another night attack and after scrambling around like goats, we reached the summit at three in the morning and took the German OP (Observation post) prisoner. The supporting

German infantry were dug in on the reverse slope, so a counter-attack came in straight away as it always was with the Germans. This was beaten off. I was as usual in 'A' company and with us were 'C' company. We had started to consolidate our position by improving our slit trenches when another counter- attack came in. This one made progress but was halted by an officer firing a Bren from the hip (Lt D.A. Main, commissioned in North Africa where he won a DCM).

Now that the op was knocked out, the tanks (6th Armoured Division) and our other companies could make progress. Our ammo and other supplies were brought up by some of our blokes (platoons of D company, 10RB, were used as porters, an arrangement which entailed a long and difficult climb to reach the forward companies) so we spent all available time improving our position which was, to say the least, precarious. As darkness fell a listening patrol went out with a radio. Their job was to warn of counter-attack and prepare for two-strong fighting patrols to advance, one from each company, to see if the Germans were still there. The Germans were still there alright. As the last of the sun set, all hell broke loose. They overran the listening patrol. One rifleman crawled back with his foot off, and later told us the man with the radio was killed outright when a German fired a Panzerfaust right at him. The Germans had crept to within about fifty yards of the riflemen then swarmed all over them.

The counter-attack was in considerable strength and was concentrated at the shoulders of the hill. This meant the Germans could drive in the companies' flanks and send them tumbling back down the hill. Then the op would be re-established and shelling of the road would recommence.

These Germans really did know their drill. They ran at you then dropped and rolled into the slit trench with you. But we had a few tricks up our sleeve. The riflemen carried No 36 grenades which they left in the bottom of the trench with the pin pulled as they rolled out. You can imagine the results. I had one German drop into my slit trench. I think he had the wind up as much as I did because we both just looked at one another. It was self-preservation for both our artillery and the Germans were by now slinging shells around. Our guns were hitting the top of the hill and sending red-hot splinters and rock flying everywhere. What with the full moon and the tracer rounds fired by the Germans, it was almost like day time. They say there is no such thing as an atheist when you are being shelled. Well I shut my eyes and uttered a little prayer. So I reckon did the German, for as the guns lifted, he rolled out without a word.

We were overmatched up on Maggio, so they withdrew the two companies back down the hill, and let the artillery have a clear go at the Germans. At first light a truce was declared and our stretcher bearers, one of their number being my future brother-in-law, went out looking for the wounded and missing. It turned out two riflemen were missing, so he strolled up to these Germans and asked if they had any rifleman as prisoners. It turned out that both were in fact prisoners, so my brother-in-law took the opportunity to offer the Germans some fags while he glanced at one of their Spandau machine gun positions. They all departed the best of friends.

We were withdrawn and replaced by the Argylls who endured a strong attack from the Germans and suffered many casualties before they (the Germans) retired to new defensive positions further north.

The terrain 100 miles north of Rome had not been nearly so favourable for defence as it had been further south and by 15 July XIII Corps had stormed Mount Ligano, the high ground which controlled the roads to Arezzo and the Germans finally withdrew. The pursuit now continued slowly northwards along the Arno River and through Chianti wine country.

The destruction of the main bridge over the Arno meant a considerable delay as they had to wait for a Bailey to be erected. While 10 RB were sent to clear the high ground so the sappers could make a start, 7RB were sent north to see if it was possible to use the intact bridge further north. Their objective was Castiglion Fibbocchi, a small, walled city that lay between Arezzo and Cortona. Situated on a hilltop and 345 metres above sea level it overlooked the Val di Chio and the Preappenines. In order to use the bridge the city would need to be in Allied hands.

It was a dark night and there was little information about either terrain or enemy presence and this led 'B' Company into a trap. As they crept forward in the darkness the company began to bunch up. Suddenly, and without warning, six Spandaus opened up from three sides. As the Germans were occupying the high ground and covering each other it was impossible to take them so 'B' company began a rapid withdrawal. Although several men were wounded none were killed or missing.

Fortunately it was still dark so the battalion rapidly dug in some 600 yards away from the enemy. The next day they were extremely grateful they had been able to dig in as the Germans pounded their positions mercilessly with shells and mortars. 'A' Company worked their way round on the left flank of the enemy positions and successfully reach Pt 262 which afforded them a good view of the village and the road on to it. But they too soon came under heavy artillery fire and, unable to dig in because of the rocks, they were forced to withdraw. Deciding that the enemy position could be outflanked anyway when the main bridge was complete Divisional Command decided there was no point in continuing the difficult frontal assault; 7RB now withdrew back to positions guarding the Arno crossings:

> We prepared to cross yet another river. Our battalion came forward at first light with 'A' company in the lead. As usual we dug slit trenches just in case and nobody bothered with the entrenching tool, preferring a pick and shovel instead. The infantry sections never went anywhere without their shovels and we picked up these tools as we went. You broke the ground up with the pick then shovelled out the earth. It was a case of 'Dig or die' as we used to say in Italy. Early morning mist covered our

approach, so as some of the blokes brewed up, others started digging. From my time in the building trade, I always threw the spoil from the trench over my left shoulder, today for some reason I threw it cack-handed over my right shoulder.

All was quiet; not a sound, only blokes digging or chatting among themselves. The Guards were out in front so no one expected what happened next. As the mist cleared there was a bang and an air burst almost at once appeared over the company area. It was black, so it was one of Ted's. He'd got the range and then this artillery fire came down like rain.

All the blokes scattered as shells landed. The slit trenches were down about waist deep; enough to shelter in. A shell exploded some way away from me and a fragment dug itself into the spoil I had thrown to my right. Just think if I had thrown it to my left, as usual, then this lump of shell would have cut me in half.

Casualties mounted as the shelling increased. There must have been an OP somewhere. Horace Cann[1], one of the original battalion from the Alamein days, ran to help a bloke who was wounded. I watched from my trench as Corporal Cann pulled out a shell dressing. Then in a flash both he and the wounded rifleman disappeared, both blown to bits by a direct hit.

If we'd stayed put the company would have been destroyed so Bombhead came forward and ordered us to make a break for it and pull back over a crest to our rear. The shelling went on for the rest of the day. It wasn't the Guards to our front but the Germans. We had fifty casualties which the battalion, let alone 'A' company, could ill afford. It was only after the Germans withdrew that we crossed the river and headed off towards Arezzo.

The 5th Army reached Arno on 23 July but then, like the 8th Army to the east of them, came to a halt because of a shortage of supplies – mainly artillery shells and petrol. The Germans had totally destroyed the port at Livorno before they retreated so the Allies' supply lines were stretched and getting longer. The enforced rest allowed the men who had been fighting almost constantly since May to catch up on some much-needed relaxation in preparation for the assault on the Gothic Line. But it also wasted several weeks of good weather, something that would have disastrous consequences for the Allied advance later in the year.

Again the men made the most of the opportunity to rest. On 26 July the King visited and 500 men from the Brigade, mainly 7RB, lined the route south of Arezzo and cheered him:

> On 26 July His Majesty the King came to see the troops at Arezzo. They had a whip round in 61st Infantry Brigade and took nearly all our battalion to go and see the king. We were taken out of the line, given a change of clothes and told to stand on the side of the road and wait for the king. If the Germans had found out, they could have driven all the way back to Rome through the gap we left in our lines. Anyway we stood on the road like lemons until the king drove past, gave three cheers, then marched back up the front picking up all our kit on the way.

The enemy continued to retreat, albeit slowly and the Allies continued to pursue them. The next defensive line was the Paula Line which was opposite the town of Figline. The Allies broke through and by 29 July 2RB had pushed forward through the hilly countryside into Castelfranco and were heading towards Faella. The pursuit continued apace, always seemingly up hill, across rivers, streams and dykes, and under almost constant heavy, unnervingly accurate, shelling and mortaring. Not only were they subject to this continual bombardment, they also had to watch out for snipers and the various booby traps and mines left by the retreating Germans. Casualties continued to be very heavy and totally disproportionate to the amount of ground taken.

After some heavy fighting alongside the fast-flowing Resco River, a 7RB patrol managed to eliminate a Spandau post. This allowed them to make several successful reconnaissance patrols across the river. Things were looking up. But without warning the situation suddenly changed and instead of decreasing, enemy resistance began to stiffen. As they approached the river they were greeted by intense Spandau fire. Far from withdrawing the Germans appeared to have come forward during the night.

The fighting grew steadily worse and 7RB found themselves under heavy fire of all kinds including Nebelwefers.[2] By the end of the night the Germans had inflicted twenty-nine casualties on them. To try and provide them with some protection, 10 RB were ordered to tackle the steep sandstone cliffs and take the high ground on the right. Having successfully engaged the enemy at close quarters they managed to take three prisoners. From them they discovered that German 1 Para Division had now left and were heading to the Gothic Line leaving behind 715 Division and 334 Division to provide the rearguard.

'A' Company of 10RB, who were slightly further to the right, soon found themselves in even more trouble than 7RB. Under fire in open ground at the approach to the cliffs they discovered they were in a field of 'S' mines. 'B' Company coming up close behind found themselves in exactly the same predicament. Any attempt by the men to remove the mines was countered by the Germans who shelled them relentlessly. They also came under continuous Spandau and mortar fire. The only way out was by the road which was also heavily mined. Unable to move they remained trapped under fire for an entire day taking very heavy casualties.

As the fighting continued for several more days the weather remained extremely hot, adding to their discomfort. By the end the Brigade had taken over 100 casualties and had little to show for it.

On 2 August the Guards were moved up and took control of the area and the Brigade spent the next twenty-four hours in reserve. But the rest was short lived as they were quickly informed that the Germans had withdrawn back further and 2RB were immediately returned to the frontline where they advanced towards Castelfranco and then on to Reggelo. Patrolling by the rest of the Brigade was now increased and prisoners were regularly bought back. 7RB even

95

managed to bring back an entire enemy recce patrol of three men one day:

> Most of the villages in Italy cling to the sides of the mountains. It's been like this since the Middle Ages and it makes taking them a bind. On the occasion you do run into a village on the flat it has to be approached with great care.
>
> We did a listening patrol further up north – I can't remember the village's name – and ended up on the outskirts in the cemetery. It was misty about this time of year, so we crept into the graveyard and took cover behind some of the stones. Most of the burials were in the walls but the place had been shelled quite a bit and all the coffins and their contents were strewed all over the ground. We knew Ted also crept about in the cemetery and sure enough we had just made ourselves comfortable when one of his patrols came in. The mist had lifted a bit so all you could see were these Ted's boots and legs moving around until they found a place to hide. Nothing ever came of these patrols except losing a night's kip, but you did get the wind up when your imagination started to play tricks on you.

With the Germans now preparing themselves for the assault on the Gothic Line, the mortaring and shelling began to slacken off. The brigades took the opportunity to spend some time in the local towns and villages. The weather was still dry, hot, and sunny and the battalions ran camps for one company at a time on the north shore of Lake Trasimene. After so long fighting the men were exhausted and the chance to rest and recuperate was eagerly taken as was the opportunity to fraternize with the young ladies in the local towns and villages.

But it was not just the opportunity to enjoy themselves. It also made them feel more civilized after so many months of continual fighting. Just as in Egypt and Tunisia the Brigades had their own preferences and specific territories; 2RB headed towards Reggelo

96

while 7RB seemed to prefer the small village of Faella. After months of fighting Faella seemed particularly bright and clean after some of the places they had passed through and the inhabitants were always delighted to see them and make them welcome.

But the rest would not last long. Operation Mallory Major had begun. The plan was to demolish every bridge across the Po River and its tributaries and to target railways north and south of the river. By the beginning of August every bridge across the Po had been destroyed. The only way for the Germans to get equipment across was to use ferries or hastily constructed pontoons at night. All roads and rails west were also damaged or destroyed isolating Genoa. All routes to France had been closed and the Brenner Pass through the Alps was also blocked. This successfully reduced the Germans' ability to resupply their troops.

By 3 August the South Africans had broken through to the southern outskirts of Florence. Kesselring ordered his troops back across to the northern side of the Arno and gave the order to blow up the bridges across the river. In one large, deafening explosion all the bridges were destroyed except one fourteenth-century bridge, the Ponte Vecchio. This was too narrow to accommodate vehicles and in any case it was blocked at either end by mounds of rubble put there specifically to prevent anyone using it. The Allies were now unable to cross the river and for the next few days were harassed and shot at by snipers and held up by a small regiment of Fallschirmjaeger who had been left behind to give the rest of the army time to withdraw back to the Gothic Line.

On 4 August not long after British forces reached the Arno River, General Leese suggested that given the 8th Army's armoured superiority his forces should attack up the Adriatic coast towards Rimini. The US 5th Army had recently lost seven divisions including the experienced mountain troops of the French Expeditionary Corps to Operation Anvil, now renamed Operation Dragoon[3] – the invasion of southern France. The plan was that having drawn the German units away from the 5th Army front, General Clark could then use his more limited force to assault the Gothic Line from Florence north towards Bologna. This would allow their combined armies to converge on Bologna, encircle the Axis forces in the Po Valley and then move into the Balkans and Danube Valley. This was codenamed Operation Olive.

General Clark agreed but asked for control of XIII Corps to enhance his own troops' capability. Although General Leese objected to placing British troops under US Control Field Marshal Alexander over ruled him:

> With the invasion of southern France the Anglo-American Armies in Italy – now known as 15th Army Group – lost seven divisions, among them several crack American and French divisions. Those left were still expected to carry on regardless. Our corps, the 13th, found itself transferred from 8th to the 5th Army. We stayed part of the 5th for the next nine months.

Given the speed of the Allied advance, Kesselring had begun to have serious doubts about whether he could stop them north of Florence and the Arno. By now they were retreating rapidly towards the last real line of defence and it was by no means complete. But then lack of equipment and men forced the Allies to stop in late July and Kesselring breathed a sigh of relief. The halt had given the Germans the time they needed to speed up the strengthening of the defences along the Gothic Line. His chances of stopping the Allied advance, or at least delaying it until the weather broke, had just increased dramatically.

Notes
1. Corporal Horace Cann was a keen photographer and it is likely it was he who took the photograph of Henry by the Bren gun carrier.
2. Known as 'Smoke mortars' there were initially two different types before they were replaced by a variety of rocket launchers ranging in size from 15 to 32cm (5.9 to 13in). The thin walls of the rockets had the great advantage of allowing much larger quantities of high explosives to be delivered than artillery or even mortar shells of the same weight.
3. Apparently because the British had been 'dragooned' into going along with it.

Chapter 10

The Gothic Line

The Gothic Line was the final defensive line which ran from Pesaro south of Bologne on the Adriatic and along the top of the Apennine Mountains to Massa Carrara on the Tyrrhenian Sea. In June 1944 Hitler had ordered Kesselring to rename it the Green Line because he was concerned that if the Allies did manage to overrun the German defences while it was called by its historic name, it would allow them to magnify their victory even more. The Allies, however, continued to refer to it as the Gothic Line.

The northern Apennines form an arc from the Ligurian Alps north of Genoa south-eastwards across virtually the entire peninsula to the Adriatic coast just south of Rimini. Here they turn south and become the Central Apennines. The northern face of the Apennines is gentle and slopes gradually down to the Po Valley and Lombardy Plain. The southern-facing side is a totally different proposition, with steep, rugged cliffs that drop sharply into the Arno Valley and a narrow coastal plain. Erosion from the numerous streams that cross the terrain as they drain the slopes have cut irregular spurs and left sharp isolated peaks that sometimes reach as high as 6,000ft. Although the average height of the cliffs is about 3,000ft, this is still a steep rise from the Lombardy Plain which is about 300ft above sea level.

Most of the streams run in the same direction, either north-east to the Po Valley or south to the Arno River or Ligurian Sea. The deep valleys cut by these rivers and streams, combined with the irregular geology of the range, divide the North Apennines into numerous compartments which provide excellent natural defensive positions.

In 1944 the only routes between villages were simple dirt tracks used by carts or mule trails, neither of which were suitable for the movement of either wheeled or tracked vehicles.

Spread across the lower slopes of the mountains were grain fields, vineyards and olive groves, whilst areas across the upper slopes that had not been eroded were covered by forests of chestnuts, oak and evergreens. Where erosion had taken place there were bare rock slopes, sheer cliffs and steep ridges.

The lower slopes of the Apennines north of Florence extend almost as far as the Arno River. To the west these foothills curve north-eastwards rising above the river plain. The Monte Albano ridge rises to a height of 2,014ft, fifteen miles west of Florence, while the 3,000ft Monte Pisano ridge lies four miles north-east of Pisa. The many roads that linked the towns and villages across the plain were themselves criss-crossed by numerous drainage canals.

There were twelve all-weather roads that crossed the Apennines to the Po Valley and Lombardy plain but of these only five were suitable for large scale military operations and led to points of strategic importance. There were also several secondary roads that wound their way across the mountains and through the narrow valleys to the Po Valley. However these roads were very narrow in places. They also had numerous bends and curves and steep gradients. There were few bridges and there were few alternative crossings that could be used during the frequent landslides caused by the heavy rains that blocked the roads.

In September these rains would turn the streams into raging torrents that flooded roads and washed away the few bridges. With the rains came thick, swirling mists that seeped down from the mountains and filled the valleys, reducing visibility to virtually nothing. Higher up the slopes in October the snows would come. They froze the air and periodically blocked the mountain passes.

There were even fewer roads available to the Allies south of Arno and those that did exist were generally in a poor state of repair because of heavy German military traffic that had used it. On the whole the roads available to the US 5th Army in the western sector were better than those available to the British 8th Army east of the Central Apennines and they were also less prone to ice and snow than those on the east. Two of Italy's best railways were also on the west coast of the Apennines and could deliver an estimated 10,000 tons of supplies daily if necessary. The only railway on the east coast was a single track line which at peak capacity could only deliver an estimated 3,000 tons daily.

The valleys, road and railway network meant the Germans had much shorter supply lines than the Allies. They also controlled Highway 9 which ran from Rimini in the west to Milan in the centre of the region and linked Cesena, Forli, Bolgna, Modena, Reggio and Parma. But Allied air superiority was causing them serious problems, especially with the railroads. All the frontier lines entering Italy converged at the foot of the Alps after crossing through vulnerable alpine passes. The junctions at Genoa, Turin, Milan, Verona, Trieste and Mestre were the distribution points for the rest of Italy. All German supplies and troops coming via the Alps came through these junctions. Destruction of any of these junctions would seriously disrupt Italy's north-south as well as the east–west traffic, especially as the Italian railways had very few loops for avoiding these junctions.

The Gothic Line itself was a series of defences woven into the hills and mountains of the Apennines, exploiting the natural features of the terrain which favoured the defender. It was 180 miles long and several miles deep, and was filled with Panther gun turrets, steel shelters, defensive positions dug deep into the rocks and extensive minefields and wire emplacements. There were 2,376 machine-gun posts, 479 anti-tank guns plus other mortar and assault guns positions, thousands of field fortifications made of rock, wood, steel and steel girded concrete, 120,000 metres of wire, and many miles of anti-tank ditches such as the one at Santa Lucia near the Futa Pass. In front of it was another security line and 20km behind it was the Gothic Line 2.

Fortunately for the Allies, construction work was still incomplete. It had originally been scheduled for completion in December but given the speed of the Allied advance work, had been speeded up. The Todt organisation had quickly conscripted thousands of Italians in an attempt to finish before the Allies reached it. However the need to complete it in a hurry meant they were less careful about whom they 'employed'. Amongst those they conscripted were many partisans who soon found ingenious ways to sabotage the line. Emplacements were built with blind traverses and the pill boxes were constructed in such a way that they didn't quite command a full view all around. In addition, much of the cement that came from the Italian mills was of poor quality and workers were slow and lethargic, all of which would aid the Allies in their advance.

Meanwhile, whilst his troops were retreating, Kesselring had ordered an operation to clear the Apennines of partisans who were now causing a serious problem for the retreating troops. But the partisans refused to engage in full battle, preferring to take pot shots and then disappear back into the mountains. Frustrated that they were unable to destroy them, the Germans took their revenge on the villages and towns by burning buildings, executing civilians and taking hostages. Several massacres of men women and children took place by both German and GNR[1] troops.

At the same time in the Apuan Mountains north of Lucca, the Germans began the forced evacuation of civilians from the valleys and mountains. The reasoning behind the clearance was two-fold. First it was thought that with no civilians in the area offering aid and support to the partisans it would be harder for them to operate, thus when the battles for the Gothic line began they would be less able to interfere. Secondly once the battles began it would be no place for civilians.

But those living in the mountains and valleys did not want to move and a delegation of local parish priests was sent to try and persuade the Germans not to evacuate the area. Their arguments fell on deaf ears but then the local partisan group, The Apuan Patriots, began ordering the civilians not to leave. The situation rapidly worsened when the 10th Garibaldi Brigade who operated in the Apuans managed to prevent a German clearance of the area for two days on 30/31 July and then put up posters in Sant'Anna boasting about their success and telling civilians to ignore the evacuation order and stay where they were.

1. The GNR were a fascist militia that had replaced the Black Shirts and were used mainly as an anti-partisan force.

By 12 August the Tenth Garibaldi Brigade had moved elsewhere and Sant'Anna and Stazzema were swollen with refugees. The Germans now considered them to be centres of partisan resistance and so ordered in the 34th Panzer Grenadiers to clear the area. These frontline troops, battle hardened from their fighting in Russia, herded the population into barns while their houses were burned down. Grenades were then thrown into the barns and machine guns fired indiscriminately at the unarmed civilians. As the guns fell silent the barns were set on fire, ensuring that those not already dead were burned alive. In all, 560 men women and children of all ages were killed in a horrific bloodbath.

The Allies were totally unaware of the massacre that was happening just a few miles ahead. Their biggest problem at that time was how to deceive Kesselring that the main thrust of the attack was still towards Florence. Although there was an almost total lack of enemy air reconnaissance, moving the British troops across Italy from the central area to the Adriatic without drawing attention was still fraught with difficulty and meant using circuitous routes over battle-scarred land and through the mountains. The transfer of small groups began on 15 August and took place mainly at night. Despite the difficulty, it only took eight days to redeploy eleven divisions and nine separate brigades to the twenty-five- mile wide Adriatic front.

To continue the deception, Alexander decided to make it appear that the 5th and 8th Armies were moving routinely towards the Gothic Line without any particular combat plan. Once the Polish II Corps came close to the Gothic Line the reserve forces behind them would launch a lightening attack which would break through the defences. By then, the 5th Army should have crossed the Arno and be in a position to attack the Gothic Line north of Florence.

Intercepted radio reports indicated that the Germans had no idea about the change of tactics or that an attack along the coast was imminent.

On 25 August Operation Olive began with the first phase being to take Rimini. The battle was fought by 1,200,000 men, thousands of guns, tanks and aircraft, and was one of the biggest to take place in Italy. As the sound of the guns echoed through the mountains, reverberating off the peaks and shaking the ground, it reminded Henry of giant thunderstorms, rumbling and groaning across the sky. The flashes of the artillery, mortars and other weapons lit up the sky relentlessly; their strikes on the German defences like giant lightning bolts. It was something that those who took part would never forget and whenever Henry heard thunder he would find himself inevitably drawn back to the battles for Italy.

The British 5th Corps and Canadian 1st Corps attacked through two Polish divisions on a seventeen-mile-wide front along the Adriatic while supported by the British Desert Air Force. They made good progress as Kesselring had originally believed the 8th Army assault was a diversion and delayed reinforcing his coastal units for four days, even though the Poles and Canadians had breached the line near Pesaro on 30 August. But despite this success the Allies were unable to mobilise their armoured units fast enough. This allowed Kesselring to plug the gap and at the same time inflict 8,000 casualties on the attacking forces. By September the 8th Army had been halted short of taking Rimini and the Romagna Plain. But despite this setback Alexander was sure that the 5th Army attack on the second front would succeed.

General Clark planned to open his phase of Operation Olive on 10 September 1944 with an assault by all three corps under his command. On the left were the US IV Corps which consisted of the US 1st Armored Division, the South African 6th Armoured Division and 2 Regimental Combat Teams, the US 92nd Infantry Division (Buffalo Soldiers) and the Brazilian 6th RCT. In the centre was the US II Corps which consisted of the US 34th, 85th, 88th and 91st Infantry Divisions supported by three tank battalions. On the right was the British XIII Corps consisting of the British 1st Infantry Division, 6th Armoured Division, 8th Indian Division and 1st Canadian Tank Brigade.

The weakest point of the Gothic Line from the German point of view was the Futa Pass. To rectify this, two of the five divisions who were covering the whole of the Apennines Sector were sent to defend it. As well as the 5km anti-tank ditch, the other defences included concrete pillboxes and Panther tank turrets with 75mm guns plus minefields and barbed-wire entanglements. Because of this Clark decided to break though at the lesser defended Il Giogo Pass from which he could then outflank the Futa Pass. However to achieve this they would first need to take the high ground, the Monticelli hill mass on the left of Highway 6524, and Monte Altuzzo on the east.

The plan was for II Corps to advance along the road from Florence to Firenzuola and to Imola through the Il Giogo pass which would allow them to outflank the heavy defences at the Futa Pass on the main Florence – Bologna Road. On their right XIII Corps would advance through the Gothic Line to cut Route 9 at Faenza.

As August drew to a close the US II Corps and British XIII Corps began to move into the mountains to take up their positions. Although they met fierce resistance from some of the outposts, by the end of the first week in September the Germans began to withdraw.

However, although they were now withdrawing from the out-skirts of Florence, as usual they had left booby traps and other delaying tactics behind. The villages round Pontassieve had been heavily planted with mines and these caused several casualties:

> Booby traps were a menace in Italy. Ted took it to an art form and he might slow you up or inflict casualties any time. The myth says that a shell will never land again in an old shell hole but whoever said that did not have to contend with the Germans in Italy. Our company took over a position near the Gothic Line; the place had been heavily shelled and there were shell holes everywhere. A section of our blokes took shelter along the rim of one big shell crater and as was usual the Germans started shelling the position, so an officer decided to make himself scarce and jumped over the riflemen on the lip and into the bottom of the crater to escape the incoming shells. What he did not know, nor did anyone else as a matter of fact, was that the Germans had left an 'S' mine in the bottom. The officer set the mine off, which killed him outright and badly wounded the blokes around the lip. The stretcher bearers went and picked up the officer. Such was the power of the 'S' mine that he had upwards of twenty ball bearings in

him and the blood just poured out through the bottom of the stretcher. From then on we always had a look in the bottom of shell holes.

Despite this, 2RB reached Consuma, about twelve miles up Route 70, on the evening of 27 August. Here they found the survivors of another massacre. The retreating Germans had murdered twenty women and children apparently in revenge for partisan attacks, although the villagers had no contact with any partisans and had no idea why they had been targeted.

As usual the bodies had been left where they had fallen, presumably as a warning to the partisans and the men spent several hours burying them, all the time keeping watch for any rear guard troops, mines, booby traps and snipers. Burying bodies of civilians, especially children, was particularly unpleasant but as these had been there some days this was a particularly horrible task. The survivors, who were hiding in the remaining buildings, were given medical treatment and food before they moved on.

Then 7RB were moved up to take over this sector with the Lothians and 16/5th Lancers and continued the advance. Two miles further on they made contact with the Germans and picked up a German sergeant and another soldier who had been trying to set up an Observation Post on the very hill that 7 RB had secured during the night. The advance continued and it looked as if they might finally have the Germans on the run. But by now it was September and the weather began to turn.

After the hot, dry, dusty heat of the past few months, the rain was initially welcome as it cooled the air making conditions a lot more comfortable as they climbed ever upwards. But as it grew heavier and more persistent it began to turn the grassy mountain slopes into slippery muddy tracks impeding the advance. It also reduced visibility and made it harder to spot the booby traps, hidden snipers and all the other dangers. As they went higher into the mountains the rain turned icy and the conditions deteriorated even more. The hail stones bounced off their inadequate summer uniforms and soaked them through to their skin. As the hail and rain fell relentlessly it caused mists and fog that swirled round them,

106

disorientating them, and as it fell on the bare slopes they became even more slippery, causing them to stumble and lose their footing:

> Passing north-east of Florence we began to reach the outer defences of the Gothic Line which ran diagonally from Rimini to Pisa. The weather began to turn in September, but this did not stop 15th Army Group mounting Operation Olive. The part played by 5th Army became known in history as the Battle of the Passes, as the Americans, with British 13 Corps, tried to reach Bologna and the plain of Lombardy before the winter snows covered the Apennine Mountains.

The 5th Army's main assault with II Corps began at dusk on 12 September after a heavy artillery barrage, but progress was slow. However on their right XIII Corps was making good progress so Clark took the opportunity to exploit this by bringing up the 337th Infantry from reserve. On 17 September a joint attack enabled the Allies to fight their way onto Monte Pratone which was a key position on the Gothic Line and only two or three miles east of the Il Giogo pass. At the same time II Corps renewed their assault on Monte Altuzzo on the east side of the pass and this too fell on 17 September after five days of intense fighting. The Il Giogo Pass finally fell on 22 September. Meanwhile, on 18 September XIII Corps' 8th Indian Infantry had taken the heights of Femminamorta while and the 6th Armoured Division took the San Godenzo Pass on Route 67 to Forli:

> But in the end the weather and the Germans prevented the Americans from achieving their objective, while 8th Army captured Rimini and then fought a series of small actions to improve their position and thus breeched the Gothic Line.

From 22 September to the end of the month, II Corps units only managed to push six to eight miles closer to the Po Valley. The bad weather that had already slowed Eighth Army's advance farther east now began to slow the 5th Army's advance. The torrential rains began swelling the rivers and streams which washed away bridges and turned the tracks into quagmires that reduced troop and supply movements and made them increasingly treacherous. Thick swirling fogs and mists dramatically reduced visibility. Replacements for the 2,150 casualties were slow in coming and enemy resistance began to stiffen, finally forcing Clark to abandon his attack on Imola on 1 October, just twelve miles from his objective. Instead, he moved II Corps toward Highway 65 and replaced it with elements of the British XIII Corps.

As the Allies had crept slowly forward the partisans had also increased their activity behind enemy lines. Determined to wipe out the partisans once and for all, the Germans now prepared an attack on Monte Sole. But it was not just the partisans that the Germans killed. Between 22 and 29 September the Marzabotto massacre took place. Figures of the dead continue to be disputed but it is agreed that anything between 770 and 1,000 people, mainly men, women and children including babies were killed in the worst massacre in western Europe in the Second World War. Hand grenades were thrown into schools, churches and houses, and those who survived the initial onslaught were machine gunned. Those who survived only did so because they were buried under the corpses of their own families, relatives and friends. This murder of the civilian population of Marzabotto and the surrounding villages was carried out by units of the 16th Waffen SS Panzer Grenadier Division under the orders of SS *Sturmbannführer* Walter Reder. They were the same units who had carried out the previous murders in Sant'Anna and Stazzema on 12 August.

Meanwhile, the continuous fighting began to take its toll on the men. It was not just the fighting that was affecting them. Advancing towards an isolated village or farmhouse they became accustomed to finding the rotting corpses of civilians barely hidden from view; a result of the numerous calculated massacres intended to reduce partisan activity in the area. Surrounded by so much horror, it was not surprising that they began to withdraw from their friends. Henry now became convinced that his time was up. Especially prior to the next planned assault when they were told yet again that the

108

opposition, if any, was likely to be 'a rusty Spandau and few tired "Eyties"'.

> Blokes react defiantly when they are frightened or wounded. One bloke went bomb happy before our first attack in Italy when someone had one up the spout and let a round off behind this youngster. He went straight into shock and was carted off. Another NCO was hit in the head by a shell fragment about the size of a pea. He had been wearing a tin hat and the fragment spun around inside, split the liner and cut one of his ears. From that day onwards he showed everyone the effects the fragment had on his helmet and his ear. What we could not see was the effect of his mind. Every day we had a visit from a German aircraft spotting for his artillery and this NCO was convinced the German pilot could see him and he would get out his rifle, fire a round at the aircraft which was well out of range, then after pulling it through, replace the rifle in its slip. After a while this started to get on everyone's wick, so one of the officers sent him back with battle fatigue.
>
> When a bloke is wounded his reaction is surprising. One in particular was hit in the chest during an attack but instead of going down he got up and ran around in circles then shot off towards our own lines. The carriers were dismounted at this time, so me and another carrier driver, Freddie Arnold, tore off and caught him. Freddie offered to take him back to the regimental aid post and was promptly put on a charge for leaving the frontline. This was later dismissed.
>
> Planning for the next attack was suspect and the opposition was expected to be 'a rusty Spandau and a few tired Eyties'. The attack was meant to go on at last light so the attacking company cooled its heels for the whole day. The atmosphere was very oppressive and I kept remembering other riflemen who, in the desert, sought their own company and kept away from their comrades before a battle and who subsequently hadn't come back. I too found myself keeping

my own counsel and becoming increasingly more anxious. It was a relief when a Don R (dispatch rider) came up and told the Colonel the attack was off and the company was to stay where it was. Another regiment was to carry out the attack.

Later we heard rumours that the battalion of the other regiment sent to attack this position had come under withering fire and lost many men. So much for the rusty Spandau!

The 6th Armoured Division had been redirected towards Imola. The main feature of the area was a ridge that ran from the Santerno to Monte Taverna and then away towards Battaglia. On 26 October 'A' Company were redirected to Mt Taverna which was the next dominating feature and 'B' Company 7RB pushed forwards Osara. It was a pitch-black night and the going was increasingly difficult so by the morning only the lower slopes had been reached. The Company dug in and waited for the night to come so they could resume their assault. However, the heavy defences that were in place had been overlooked and they came under extremely heavy, very accurate, shelling and mortaring. The attack was called off and the company was finally withdrawn after taking appalling casualties.

Chapter 11

Hypothermia, Summer Uniforms and Food Poisoning

Despite the continuing bad weather, on 1 October Clark ordered II Corps to advance up Highway 65, supported by 6th South African Armoured and US 1st Armored Divisions on the left flank and the British 78th (transferred from 8th Army) on the right. They advanced only four miles in three days and took over 1,730 casualties as German resistance stiffened and the weather and terrain worsened. Between the 5 October and 9 October the 5th Army only advanced another three miles at the cost of 1,400 casualties.

The final phase of the assault began on 10 October as they attacked the ten- mile-long Livergnano Escarpment which was a steep line of solitary mountain peaks running east-west and forming the enemy's strongest natural defensive position in the northern Apennines.

For the first time in a week the weather had cleared enough to use air support provided by the Mediterranean Allied Tactical and Strategic Air Forces (MATAF and MASAF) in an operation called Operation Pancake. In the ground attacks that followed the air assault the 85th Division succeeded in taking Monte delle Formiche on 10 October and the 91st Division outflanked the Livergnano Escarpment from the west. The German forces finally withdrew on 13 October but the worsening weather, difficult terrain and fierce resistance finally halted the advance just ten miles south of Bolgna.

Field Marshal Alexander now decided to use the Fifth and Eighth Armies together to make another attempt at capturing Ravenna and

111

Bologna. Under this plan, the Fifth Army would break out of the Apennines and encircle the German X Army from the north-west, while the Eighth Army continued along the east along the Adriatic. But supply lines now stretched back many miles across the rugged mountain terrain and the weather was gradually closing in.

The Germans were also facing problems. Although Kesselring wanted to retreat back to the Alps, Hitler had ordered him to stand firm so he reinforced the line with his two reserve units, the 16th Waffen SS Panzer Grenadier and 94th Infantry Divisions.

The US 34th Division tried to break through to Bologna on 16 October but the advance was quickly halted by a combination of fierce enemy opposition and difficult terrain. Even with XIII Corps holding down the German 334th, 715th, and 305th Infantry Divisions the 91st and 1st Armored could not advance any further. All hope of a quick breakthrough was finally extinguished when Kesselring reinforced the line with the 29th and 90th Panzer Grenadier Divisions.

On 27 October, General Sir Henry Maitland Wilson, the Supreme Allied Commander in the Mediterranean, had no option but to order a halt to further major offensives. Priority given to combat operations in northern Europe meant the resupply of troops with 'munitions and other items was intermittent. Even slower was the arrival of new troops to replace the growing casualties. The troops on the frontline were now totally exhausted and enemy resistance seemed to be growing rather than decreasing. The weather was rapidly deteriorating.

Despite this decision both armies were then ordered to attempt a further assault on the German defences so Field Marshal Alexander ordered the 15th Army to rotate units from the front so they could rest and retrain ready for another offensive on 15 November. Clark was able to comply quite quickly, having just received 3,000 replacements, although he was still short of 7,000 men. The 8th Army was now to attack Imola and Budrio and head north towards Ravenna, thus drawing enemy units away from the Bolgna front. Once they had taken Imola or by 7 December – whichever came first – Clark's II Corps would launch their assault providing the weather permitted.

112

The battalion had a rest area at Passignano and Morocco, south of Florence and on the Siena road. Here they left their heavy kit, anti-tank guns and carriers, and various other things that were no longer needed on the frontline. As they would come back here every three weeks over the next few months it soon became like a home-from-home.

Despite the halt to large-scale major operations, patrolling had continued unabated. These took place whatever the weather. On one such patrol Henry and his fellow riflemen came across a pig:

> On one patrol we took shelter in a sty to avoid the foul weather. The farmer must have left in a hurry because he left two pigs behind. The heat from the animals in the shelter kept us warm, but the Germans must have had the same idea because some of the mountain troops took up residence later that night. No one noticed until the Germans began to herd off one of the pigs at first light. We looked over our sty wall just as they were leaving. Both sides looked at one another; a couple of the Germans waved and then we took their pig off them. I don't think for one minute either side even thought about firing.
>
> Having liberated the pig in autumn, we then kept it in the back of a three-tonner and fed it scraps. In the run up to Christmas 1944 I butchered it. I was the only man with the experience so I hung the dead pig up and, with all the blokes watching me, cut it open and pulled the guts out to give to the Italians. All the blokes, veterans of such battles as Alamein, Mareth and the Arno Valley, felt queasy and walked off. We all enjoyed eating it though, especially the officers!

By the end of November 'C' Company had moved forward to Fontanelice which was heavily mined and full of booby traps. Penzula was taken a few days later and the whole battalion then moved into the Fontanelice area, their frontline situated on a ridge on the other side of the village. Preparations were now made to take

113

to Tossignano, a large village perched on a hill overlooking the Brigade sector.

On 15 December several changes of leadership took place after the death of the chief of the British Military Mission in Washington, Field Marshal Sir John Dill. Field Marshal Alexander was appointed Supreme Allied Commander in the Mediterranean in place of General Wilson who went to Washington to replace Dill. General Clark took command of the 15 Army Group in place of Alexander, while Major General Lucian K. Truscott Jr., returned from France to head the Fifth Army. General Sir Richard L. McCreery, who replaced General Leese as Eighth Army commander on 1 October, remained in command of that force.

Changes had also taken place within the Axis forces as Field Marshal Kesselring had been injured on 23 October when his staff car had collided with an artillery piece being towed along a crowded mountain road. General Vietinghoff became commander of Army Group C until he was transferred to the Eastern Front in late January. He then returned in March 1945 to replace Kesselring permanently.

Meanwhile preparations to take Tossignano had continued. The plan was to send 7RB in on a diversionary attack while 2RB would carry out the main attack; 'B' Company 7RB advanced and success-fully occupied Cogalina and Montecchio while 'C' Company 7RB advanced towards Borgo Tossignano. Both operations were carried out in silence and were completely successful. After this, 10RB moved forward to relieve them and they returned back to the rest area:

> The shortage of men in Italy became chronic in the winter of 1944/45 and 61st Infantry Brigade was no different. Made up of three motor battalions, the brigade even at full strength was smaller than an ordinary infantry brigade. From the breakout at Monte Cassino, the brigade had fought up in the hills and mountains along the Arno Valley, then overlooking Perugia and finally into the Gothic Line. It was neither trained nor equipped for mountain fighting but somehow had succeeded in getting this far. Although

114

adequate most of the time, some of the planning for our attacks had been risky and companies found themselves in situations against superior numbers of Germans where casualties had been high. One such occasion was the attacks on Borgo Tossignano and Tossignano.

Both towns are situated on the Valley of Chalk near the approaches to the Plain of Lombardy and thus Bologna. The fair city of Bologna you will recall was the objective of the American 5th Army. Taking it would cut the German lateral lines of communications and separate the two armies facing 15th Army Group. The Germans had picked their positions well. Tossignano was in the valley and was the objective of our battalion. Above the valley, Borgo Tossingano clung to the side of a hill and was the target of the 2nd battalion. At this stage of the war 2RB were very much the worst for wear, having been abroad since the 30s. Many of the battalion's pre-war soldiers were gone and those who were left resented being used as heavy infantry. To make things worse the whole area came under the sector held by the veteran German 305th Infantry Division.

The final plan called for our battalion to attack Tossignano, and then 2RB, now supported by 10RB, would climb the hill and occupy Borgo Tossignano. I say occupy because army intelligence now thought the village empty.

Attacking Tossignano at night our battalion quickly over-ran the village. However this success meant that the Germans now concentrated on Borgo Tossignano and brought their artillery to bear. The advance by 10RB was stopped by a German self-propelled gun and the attentions of both our and the Germans' artillery. In the meantime, companies of 2RB climbed the hill and occupied Borgo Tossignano. Infantry from the 305th Division now began infiltrating back into the village. There followed a series of desperate battles as 2RB tried to hold on to the village. But isolated by the Germans, the companies were slowly overrun and forced to surrender.

Having returned back to the rest area from their successful attack on Tossignano, the men from 7RB were slowly relaxing. But their relief at surviving their operation was short lived as it was not long before the news reached them that the main attack had failed with the loss of many experienced men:

> The implications of this failed attempt were far reaching. Not only was the loss of 2RB, the heroes of Snipe, felt by the rest of 61st Infantry Brigade but an enquiry was instituted and the position visited by Field Marshall Alexander. To keep the brigade up to strength, 2RB as the regular battalion, were reformed at the price of the disbandment of 10RB, and 1 KRR came in from 1st Armoured Division.

Orders were now given for 7RB to return to the frontline. Christmas Day was celebrated two days early and they moved back into line ready to plan their offensive. This time every detail was planned. Models and photographs of the area were studied and Company commanders flew over the positions on recce flights. They were even issued with flame throwers for the first time:

> I was given a Bren carrier with one (flame thrower) on the back. I don't mind saying that I did not think much of this, so I parked the thing and walked off. The platoon sergeant asked where the vehicle was and I told him in no uncertain words that with my reputation with Bren carriers, and their attraction to the Germans, I recommend he find someone else to drive it.

Finally ready 28 December they were told the operation had been postponed for a week. The week passed and they were told it had been postponed for a few more days. It was finally called off completely because the 8th Army were unable to carry out an offensive for several months due to a lack of shells. Feelings among the men were mixed. The operation would probably have meant heavy casualties but at the same time they felt they had been cheated of their opportunity to revenge 2RB.

The 8th Army had run into stiff resistance from the 90th Panzer Grenadier and 98th Infantry Divisions. Although the Canadian 5th Armoured Division managed to enter Ravenna, the 8th Army were subsequently unable to achieve their objective, hindered by General Wilson's removal of several British and Greek units from the battlefield. These units were withdrawn as they were to be sent to Greece where a civil war had broken out after the withdrawal of the German troops. This was between the ELAS who were communist guerrillas, and the Royal Greek Army who supported the Royal family and Greek government. Concerned about the increasing Soviet influence in Western Europe, Churchill ordered The Greek Mountain Brigade and two other infantry divisions to be sent to Greece to support the Greek Royal Army.

Realising that the 8th Army's offensive was going to fail, the weather was deteriorating rapidly and the Germans had not reduced their strength in II Corps' area, the offensive was postponed and the front fell temporarily quiet.

On 26 December Axis forces launched a counter-attack called Operation Wintergewitter against the 92nd Division which was twenty miles north of Lucca. They hoped to relieve pressure on the Italian Fascist Monte Rosa Division which was struggling against the Brazilian Expeditionary Force in the east in the Upper Serchio Valley. Fortunately the Allies had intercepted radio reports that suggested a counter-attack was imminent and General Truscott had transferred the experienced 339th and 337th Regiments, 85th Division and 2nd Brigade 8th Indian Division to IV Corps so they could reinforce the more inexperienced 92nd Division. The enemy was repelled near Barga on 26 December and the following day it finally began withdrawing. After four days of intense fighting the 8th Indian Division, with the help of XXII Tactical Air command, eventually succeeded in pushing the Axis forces back to their original positions.

In late December the snow came and this reduced patrolling and ambushes even more. It was now freezing cold. The snow was several feet deep and the risk of dying from exposure was almost higher than from enemy action, especially as the men were still wearing their summer uniforms. The men dug in their positions and

117

tried to keep warm. The boredom was relieved by regular rest periods but that meant traversing the extremely dangerous icy covered roads back down the mountains to the rest area.

For Henry and the other worn-out men, the chance of any form of respite from the constant fighting was taken eagerly despite the appalling conditions. From the heat of the desert they now had to adjust to the damp of the freezing rain and snow of the mountains of Italy. With the war nearing an end the death penalty had been abolished for desertion and this added another problem to the beleaguered armies. Cases of desertion were steadily rising as men realised that they would now just be given a custodial sentence and that there was a good chance they would be pardoned pretty soon after the war had finished:

> The weather was atrocious: first the rain which washed away the engineer's bridges, then the snow deep enough to fill your pockets. One rifleman died of exposure near Borgo San Lorenzo and all modern mechanised warfare ground to a halt. The battalion was still issued their summer KD uniform so cases of hypothermia increased. When a rifleman died of exposure, the request for battledress became imperative. Rumour was that 150,000 requests were made for battledress, few of which reached the frontline troops with most going to the rear echelon troops. The rain washed away all the engineer's bridges and the mechanised formations in the army slithered to a halt.
>
> The carrier platoons were dismounted again and rejoined the infantry companies. By now, all infantry platoons were under strength so the army combed out all the base camps for reinforcements. There were no more men coming out from Britain and 8th Army had to send formations back to north-west Europe or over to Greece. So as 8th Army attacked the Gothic Line it did so with decreasing strength in man power. The same was happening to the American 5th Army, so as before, 8th Army divisions were transferred to the Americans. The Yanks were in just as bad a state as we were.

I can remember jumping in the back of a three-tonner and seeing a few new men. These were either wounded men returning, or men who had been found at base and sent forward to fill the gaps in the platoons. Most were riflemen; men from battalions which had been disbanded to create a pool of reinforcements. Within a week nearly all the new men were gone – killed, wounded or missing. The weather may have been atrocious, but the German rearguards still had to be contended with around the demolitions of any remaining bridges.

To get past these demolitions, tracks were used up in the mountains to gain observation over the German rearguards. With the wind and rain, the summer clothing, and companies operating as porters to the attackers, things went very slowly. When this position was reached, the platoons of the attacking companies were usually mortared, causing many casualties. But find these detours they would. While the Germans were concentrating on the platoons on the mountain tops, another company made a detour on the flat and took the German rearguards from behind. Once cleared, the engineers were able to construct another Bailey bridge and the tanks could then get forward. All the time these bridges would be harried by sporadic mortaring.

There was no frontline in the second winter in Italy: both armies held houses or occupied the small mountain villages. The 'no man's land' in between was patrolled as each side hoped to ambush their adversary's supply columns. The German ski troops were a handful. They moved with effortless ease around the snow fields to shoot up the columns of mules bringing food and ammo to the front and to evacuate the killed and wounded.

Behind the Anglo American Armies, the engineers worked to repair roads and bridges so that 15th Army group could go over on to the offensive in the spring. Fatigued parties of riflemen fetched and carried for the engineers, their places taken by Tanki Wallahs at the front. Snow and ice made the armoured regiment's role redundant. Apart from adding to the artillery, they had nothing to do and so the tanks decided to dismount a squadron at a time to release infantry for other tasks or a rest.

I had the job on the mule run – a round trip of fourteen miles – with the big Indian Army beasts who always had a mind of their own. The Germans delighted in the confusion they inflicted on the mule trains. A couple of rounds and a grenade saw the mules bolt with their loads deposited in the snow. In the end the animals would sense trouble in the air and refuse to move. To rectify this, the Italian muleteers with us tucked a hot spud under their tail to make them move.

One mule in particular gave us trouble. He was a huge animal with a dropped ear which made him look as if he was turning right. He was intelligent as mules went and led the columns. It was important to load him properly as an extra pound meant he would refuse to budge. With bridles and tails tied together in the end you could have a column several hundred yards long. To pick this mule train up, the escort of me and another rifleman walked a couple of miles back behind the front. The muleteers were Italian Alpini of the co-belligerent forces who were experienced in working with mules.

Even in the coldest weather soldiers were expected to keep clean. Men washed and shaved everyday so personal hygiene was important. However one officer in particular broke the mould and earned the title of the scruffiest man in the company. The adversity to water by this officer was indeed legendary. He could be seen in the company lines wearing a balaclava, greatcoat and fingerless mittens – perfect attire you may think for the cold winter weather. However this was how he dressed for most of the year round. We all agreed this was down to his public school education. This officer's servant was the exact opposite and was the smartest man in the battalion by far. The two would argue as to who would receive the most of the breakfast ration. The officer's servant usually won as he considered he did most of the work. The officer never removed a single article of clothing during his ablutions. I could mention his name but I intend to protect his family from embarrassment. You will not be surprised therefore that this officer in question was an outstanding leader of his men and well liked for all his lack of hygiene.

In January 1945 the Allies ceased large-scale operations. In addition to the atrocious weather five 8th Army divisions and 1 Corps HQ had now been moved to north-west Europe and Greece. It was therefore agreed to spend the winter defending their current positions and preparing for the spring offensive scheduled for April 1 1945. Despite two months of manoeuvring, limited offensives and heavy casualties, they were virtually no further forward than they had been in late October 1944.

It was not just the armies who were suffering in the miserable winter conditions. The civilians had their own problems with starvation, rampant inflation, an increase in black market racketeering, civil unrest and even political violence. German reprisals, revenge killings, hostage taking and the burning of their homes for the slightest infringement of the harsh occupation rules left many living in a permanent state of terror. Those living in the mountain villages in particular suffered disproportionately from German vengeance and seemingly irrational hatred for their former allies. They were also caught in the middle of the frontline fighting between the Axis and Allied forces so suffered from continual artillery bombardments, shelling, sniper activity and the indiscriminate use of mines and booby traps:

The houses held in the winter of 1944/45 were in a very sorry state. Most, if not all, were minus their roofs and what timber did remain was used as firewood. Chances to return to civilization were keenly anticipated and our battalion had billets in the small town of Sambuca Val Di Pisa. We had to feed the villagers from our own rations as the Germans had taken everything of use as they retreated. The Germans now treated the villagers as enemies and

Italy as an occupied country. Most of the men disappeared up into the mountains rather than be conscripted into the German war industries, or they joined the bands of Partisans which roamed the hills attacking German convoys or their Fascist counterparts.

I was friends with one particular family in Sambuca. They were in a bad way when we arrived, so the riflemen had a whip round and gave them our spare rations. This was in contrast to their previous existence of scavenging food from the countryside and the children going through the refuse. The family cooked the rations and then served it at the table for everyone. This was a chance to get back to some form of civilisation.

On one occasion the family prepared a pie made from fungi (mushrooms) which they consumed no effect. But the mushrooms rendered me unconscious within hours and my next port of call was the hospital in Greve. Bullshit reigned supreme at the base hospital. There were guardsmen with trench foot laying to attention on the surgeon colonel's rounds. The army suspected that with the rise in cases of trench foot, they should be considered as self-inflicted wounds. Dire consequences were threatened, but more rational consideration came to be considered with the increase in desertions as well. As my strength returned, I was given duties which included bumping the floor. Within three days of getting out of bed I was ordered back to my battalion. Traipsing through the snow with all my kit was murder and it took me several hours to make the battalion lines. When I arrived I was promptly put on a charge.

Chapter 12

A Rare Case of Live and Let Live

My Bren carrier had been taken over by another driver and failed a maintenance inspection. My name was put forward as the driver even though I was sparko in hospital. As I staggered into the battalion lines, the company sergeant major buttonholed me and told me the bad news. I had received fourteen days in my absence and was ordered to the line to Orsara and the dreaded fort. Ordered into a three-tonner off I went to the fort to serve my time. Although called the fort, it was more like a well-built farm house similar to those constructed by Mussolini in the 1930s. The loss of most of the wood left only the walls so the interior of the building was exposed to the elements. A hotly-disputed place, the battalion already had a couple of bloody noses trying to hold onto the fort and the deserted village nearby. On one occasion the platoon holding the fort was attacked and rushed outside to man defences. At this very moment the Germans mortared the area and inflicted heavy casualties. One bloke made it back inside, slid down the wall and died where he sat. Percy Cable, the mortar platoon sergeant and a mate of mine told me this story and he should know.

All this changed when Bombhead got to hear about it. First of all he ordered a Vickers machine gun to fire on fixed lines at the fort, in effect firing at his own blokes. This however did the trick and inflicted many casualties on the Germans so that they left the fort alone and concentrated on sporadic mortar attacks. He then made sure that our fighting patrols dominated the deserted village, a kind of no man's land which neither side had the desire or the men to hold. My turn at the fort coincided with a couple of German attacks using Panzerfausts, cheap hand-held anti-tank weapons, which they fired through the windows at night.

Bombhead's change of tactics caught these Germans cold as well, and one attack suffered accordingly from the Vickers. Discarded equipment and blood trails in the morning showed that the Germans now had something to think about. We also changed the guard every two hours and posted a section in front of the fort during the daylight hours. Before we were replaced, an officer from my own company visited. They were due to take over, so the officer required all the information concerning our fortnight's stay at the fort. He spotted me and was aghast at my condition. I was told to report to the MO at once. On my return to battalion lines I went in front of the company commander and explained what had happened. The case was dismissed. I never let on who was the driver, but Bombhead found out and had him up in front of him and tore this bloke off a strip.

To keep up the fighting spirit of the platoons during the long winter months a succession of fighting patrols crept into the 'no man's land' between the armies. As I have mentioned this was not a line as such but a succession of strong points based upon houses. Each side had little problem infiltrating it even when this open ground was covered by machine guns on fixed lines. The Germans were very good at infiltration tactics and caused the forward platoons many problems such as shooting up command posts from the rear, taking prisoners, and generally making a nuisance of themselves. They were at first far-better equipped than us and had snow suits, skies, and a thorough knowledge of the area. It was at this time that I took part in a patrol which was ambushed and wiped out leaving just myself and another rifleman. This man, I forget his name, received a stomach wound and could not be left to freeze to death in the snow. I therefore decided to carry him back to our lines. Picking this bloke up on my back I started off. It was first light and so we were covered by the early morning frost and mist but as the sun came up all this cleared and I should think that every German in Italy could see me struggling back towards our lines. On our journey back the war seemed to have stopped; even the artillery had a day off. I must have dropped this bloke several times because he swore at me each time. I think it was after midday when we neared our own lines. I was exhausted and cursed this bloke for being so heavy but he did not answer so I presumed he must have passed out. As I got to our outposts the blokes crept out and took the wounded man off my back and carried him back to the RAP. I collapsed in a heap and fell into an exhausted sleep. The man had died about half an hour before we reached the outposts. I spent a couple of days recovering and then it was back to the daily grind.

Another task involved the sniper sections which again, were another way of keeping up the fighting spirit among the riflemen. Compared with the Germans our training was rather ad hoc but we took every opportunity to harass them and interfered with their own preparations for the spring offensive. One of their stunts was to bring up reinforcements and ammo in an ambulance. This contravened most of the laws of war and invariably our response was to shell the vehicle in question. Or a man might use a stretcher to take ammo up and it was one of the sniper section's tasks to prevent this at any opportunity. The artillery was also involved, sending an officer to organize a shoot with a couple of us and a section as protection.

Setting off at first light we were in position as the sun rose behind us. Our task was to observe the comings and goings around a farm house at about 400 yards. Most ranges in Italy were at about 400 yards. The sight on the Short Magazine Lee-Enfield was adequate at this range so few snipers bothered with a scope; a rarity in itself. All battalion snipers were ordered to shoot to wound and this was generally observed. A soldier in this state was a nuisance as lots of men and resources were required to get him back.

It was now we realised that the Germans were using ambulances to move men and material around. One house in particular seemed to be receiving a great deal of attention and so our gunner officer requested that one round be fired for effect. This of course might give away our close proximity to the enemy but the officer considered it necessary. The round duly arrived and struck a flank wall which promptly collapsed. What seemed like dozens of 'Teds' bolted from the building and scampered off in all directions. They must have been packed in there like sardines. The gunner officer called in a stonk behind the house which arrived pronto and caused numerous casualties among the Germans. It transpired that the house had been singled out as a jump-off point for a local attack by the Germans.

We waited to see if anything else transpired and sure enough, just after midday, another German appeared from inside the house. He carried one of their long-handled spades and we all knew what he was about to do. After finishing digging a little hole for himself he drove the handle of the spade into the earth next to him, dropped his trousers and began to relieve himself. Taking up a position near the gunner officer I took a bead on our German friend. It seemed ungentlemanly to shoot a man – even at this stage of the war – with his trousers down. Our gunner officer thought otherwise and asked in a whisper if I could hit him. I nodded and waited until he had almost finished, then put a round through the spade's blade. The impact toppled the spade over and it took a few seconds to register on the German that someone had taken a pot shot at him. Then, without pulling his trousers up, he was off back to the house. Our gunner officer was in fits of laughter for some while after. It was a rare case of live and let live in the mountains of Italy in the winter of 1944.

Early in the year Clark decided to launch three small attacks to give the Allies the best starting points for their spring offensive. The first attack was by the Canadians along the Adriatic on 2 January. They quickly eliminated two enemy bridgeheads on the Senio River and then dug in for the winter. The second was called Operation Fourth Term. It took place between 4 February and 11 February and saw the 92nd Division push back the Italian fascists in the Serchio Valley area. However, although the Italian forces rapidly withdrew, they were soon replaced by German forces who immediately halted the Allied advance. Eventually they had no option but to withdraw back to their original positions, having sustained over 700 casualties in just four days.

The third attack resulted from a change of tactic. No longer was Bologna the objective of the spring offensive. The focus was now on securing exits from the Apennines to the Po Valley. The US 10th Mountain Division, who had begun arriving in Italy on 27 December 1944, set out to capture the high ground on the right wing of the IV Corps and eliminate enemy positions overlooking Allied forces so that the spring offensive could be shifted westward to bypass Bologna. Although there was only a small Axis force there, the Allies were taking no chances and the 10th Mountain Division was provided with artillery support, armour and anti-tank weapons. It received further infantry support from the Brazilian Expeditionary Force.

The first phase began on 19 February as the 10th Mountain division climbed the cliff face of Riva Ridge. It surprised the enemy forces there and forced them to retreat. The Americans went on to capture Monte Belvedere and Monte delta Torraccia by 23 February. Despite the worsening weather, on 3 March, a second 10th Mountain Division assault successfully attacked the recently reinforced German positions on ridges further to the north-east. By 5 March, the 10th Mountain Division had taken and occupied a solid line of ridges and mountain crests, giving the Allied forces excellent positions for further offensive operations in the spring.

But, other than these limited attacks, the Allies took the opportunity to rest, to receive reinforcements and stockpile munitions. By late March, the Japanese-American 442d Regimental Combat Team had returned from France and the Italian Legnano Combat Group moved from 8th to 5th Army control:

> In the spring Italian co-belligerent forces took over and the brigade returned to 8th Army command near Cattolica on the Adriatic Coast. As we drove to our concentration areas we passed through the battlefields of September where 8th Army had began its own attempt to break onto the Lombardy Plain. This by all intents and purposes had been a very bloody affair costing the Army many casualties as it attacked across a series of ridges against massed German anti-tank gun defences. We came across these Bren carriers from one of the Indian mobs who had copped it. So, always on the scrounge, Morgan told me to stop and then ordered Horace to jump out and hunt around for something useful. After a while Horace found a carrier with some tools still in the back. He rooted around and then appeared with what he said was a track wrench. Morgan was not convinced and on closer inspection told Horace that it was a human shin bone. Seems the gunner did not make it when the carrier brewed up.
>
> Rimini had fallen to the Greek Brigade, but as 8th Army fought towards San Marino the weather broke and rain turned the battlefield into mire. Still 8th Army pressed on. It was now under the command of General Sir Richard McCreery in a series of small offensives with limited objectives. Casualties remained high but the Germans were forced back into a precarious defensive position near Lake Comarcchio.
>
> By now 61st Brigade had converted back to its original role as motor battalions for the armoured regiments of 6th Armoured Division. It was broken down into regimental groups, a company of riflemen and squadron of tanks now

prepared to exploit any opening in the German defences when the last attacks of the Italian campaign were launched.

Codenamed Operation Grapeshot, 8th Army attacked through the Argenta Gap while an amphibious operation took place across Lake Commarchio supported by airborne drops. To soften up the Germans and keep them off balance, his defences underwent strong air attacks. These defences were considered impregnable. For one thing they combined river and high sand banks which were covered by artillery and machine guns. The German Infantry Divisions were somewhere near full strength and a mobile reserve waited to destroy any breakthrough by 8th Army. More importantly, 8th Army was now considered a spent force as it was tired after its advance from the Alamein Line and was short of men and equipment. Nowhere was it considered possible for 8th Army to go over to the offensive, but they did not reckon with Sir Richard McCreery who likened the 8th Army to an old steeplechaser who, with a little coaxing, could still make the final hurdle.

Intensive training took place in March and the companies of riflemen worked with the tanks. Our battalion and 17/21st Lancers formed regimental groups and practised our trade around several deserted villages behind 8th Army front; 6th Armoured went into 8th Army reserve ready to be unleashed into 'the hole' hacked into the German lines by the assaulting Infantry Divisions of 8th Army. The Germans, for their part, were blissfully unaware of the maelstrom about to be unleashed on them by 15th Army Group.

By April 1945 the Germans had two armies under the control of Colonel-General von Vietinghoff. The X Army contained four corps including the 1st Paratroop Corps and thirteen divisions including reserves. The XIV Army had four corps, one of which was the Italian Fascist Army of Liguria, thirteen divisions, plus some reserve brigades. This left them with twenty-six divisions in all, but many were considerably under strength. Thus, the Axis forces had about 500,000 troops including 45,000 Italians. They also had twenty-six tanks (all of which were on the front facing the 8th Army), 1,436 Field guns of various calibres, 400 anti-tank guns and 450 self-propelled guns. They had no air support and were short of ammunition.

In contrast, the Allied 8th Army had four corps of eight divisions, plus a number of infantry and armoured brigades and 2nd Commando Brigade, a total of about 600,000 men including reserves. The 5th Army had two corps of eight divisions, plus a number of independent tank and infantry regiments making a total of 1.3 million men. The Allies forces outnumbered the Axis forces by four to one and they had massive air and tactical support:

> The American 5th Army began the last offensive of the Italian Campaign in April 1945. Military intelligence watched the German reserve divisions and evaluated intercepts from Bletchley Park. 8th Army remained behind its start lines, happy to let the 15th Air force carry out attacks on the German defences. No attacks went in after the air sorties finished, so the Germans became accustomed to 8th Army's inactivity. Their own intelligence calculated that 8th Army was exhausted and thus unable to carry out offensive operations. 6th Armoured moved forward to the airfield at Forli and waited for their time. Still under 8th Army command, this powerful division was under the direct command of General McCreery. Another air attack went in on the German defences. This time however the forward battalions and regiments of 8th Army were massed behind the bombers and fighter bombers. As the latest sortie ebbed as usual, General McCreery let slip the leash and 8th Army attacked.

> The air force had done their job. Already German divisions trying to move position were decimated by air attack and the amphibious operation across Lake Comarcchio left 8th Army threatening the Germans' escape routes. Still however the hole did not appear in the German defences. Our battalion waited ready for the off; our target when we moved was the Po River. But before we could reach that,

there were a series of German defences concentrated on rivers which ran diagonally across our front. A truly well-prepared line of defences faced 8th Army, but we now had the equipment to deal with them.

In order to draw German reserves away from the main assault area, diversionary attacks were launched in the first week of April. In Operation Roast the British 2nd Commando Brigade together with the partisans of 28th Garibaldi Brigade and armour were sent to capture the seaward isthmus of Lake Comacchio and take Port Garibaldi on the north side of the lake. Bombing raids destroyed the Axis supply routes forcing the enemy to use sea, canals and rivers, and these routes were targeted by Operation Bowler which destroyed Axis shipping.

Heavy artillery began bombarding the Senio line on 6 April and at dusk on 9 April the 8th Indian Division, New Zealand 2nd Division and 3rd Carpathian Division attacked. After heavy fighting, in which the 8th Indian Division won two Victoria Crosses, they had reached the Santerno River by dawn on 11 April. By lunchtime on 12 April the 8th Indian Division was firmly established and the British 78th Division began its assault on Argenta. Using Indian 8th Infantry Division's bridgehead across the Santerno River as a springboard, they attacked northwards on 13 April. Their objective was to set up a bridgehead at Bastia situated in the mouth of the Argenta Gap on the Reno River. Meanwhile, the 24th Guards Brigade had launched their amphibious attack on the right of the Argenta Gap. But although they were able to gain a foothold they met stiff resistance and the attack faltered on the night of 14 April. At the same time, 78th Division was also stopped. A rethink was needed.

On their right, 56th Infantry division launched the second phase of its operation which was to threaten Argenta. It established a foothold on the Fossa Marina but was unable to take the bridge across the Fossa because of heavy enemy resistance. Although 38th Brigade had crossed the bridge at Bastia over the Reno they were subsequently beaten back by an armoured counter-attack.

131

Rather than wait for support from 167th Brigade, 78th Division's 11th Infantry Brigade were ordered to use 56th Divisions bridges.

Although the 56th Division's renewed attack on 15/16 April had failed, the continued air attacks had taken their toll and on the evening of 16 April the Guards Brigade finally took the bridge. On the west side 11th Brigade advanced across the Fossa Marina while the 2nd Battalion Lancashire Fusiliers held on to the bridge-head despite heavy fire and several counter-attacks. The Royal Engineers were now able to get their armoured mobile bridges into position to allow the supporting tanks to cross.

The advance continued apace and by 18 April they were able to take Fossa Benvignante where they captured the bridge intact. On their right, the Guards cleared Chiesa del Bando and they too had reached Fossa Benvignante. By the evening of 20 April the 6th Armoured Division had reached the Fossa Cembalina. Because the ditch was impassable to tanks the enemy had decided that here was a good place to make another stand.

As the shelling and mortaring became heavier and increasingly accurate the men had dug in with some of them using a drainage ditch for cover. The going was too bad to get the soft vehicles forward and in any case there were enemy forces scattered around including snipers. The decision was made for the two lead companies (A & C) to proceed on foot, but while they were waiting for the order to advance disaster struck as the drainage ditch was hit:

> Some of the rifleman had to be dug out from a drainage ditch when the bank collapsed. They were all tangled up in their Mossie nets, so better to be bitten to death than buried alive.

By now the Colonel had decided against advancing on foot and had found an assortment of vehicles including M10 tank destroyers and 2 Arks (Royal Engineer demolition vehicles) which he then used as troop carriers:

> When 6th armoured were given the green light our regimental group headed for the Senio River, part of the

German defences that was now in 8th Army's hands. A Bailey bridge was erected by the engineers enabling the tanks of 17/21st Lancers to cross with the carriers right behind.

The gap opened up by 'A' and 'C' Company, 17th/21st Lancers, with the help of the Sappers was sufficient for the whole of 6th Armoured Division to pass through and enable them to come up on the rear of the enemy. Their objective was the heavily-defended town of Poggio Renatico which occupied the high ground and overlooked a wide sweep of open countryside:

Our objective was Poggio Renatico and we sped off towards the town sweeping all resistance before us. The speed of our advance caught the Germans off balance. The tanks set off towards Renatico, while we scrounged every available vehicle we could find. The motor platoons were ready to follow the tanks so we told some of the riflemen to jump on and hold on.

Off we went at a right old pace with the tanks running over everything in their path, including a German field hospital which we caught on the road. The land was as flat as a pancake with Italian farm buildings just off the road. Every now and again the shutters on these building would fly open and a German would fire a Spandau or Panzerfaust at the carriers. We returned fire immediately and then the tanks would put a HE into the building and everything settled down. Soon we started to run into German armour left behind by the speed of our advance. One Tiger waddled out from behind a building and took a shot at one of the Shermans. He missed, but all the Shermans, about ten I think, opened fire and the Tiger backed off as the house received several direct hits. Some of the carriers were now spinning off the road to pick up German stragglers. They would appear with sometimes thirty Teds in tow and hand them on to the Riflemen coming up behind. We reached

133

Renatico at last light, the tanks went into leaguer, and the motor platoons spent the night guarding the tanks and keeping the Germans bottled up in the town.

'A' company was given the task of getting a foothold in the town. The attack was to go in at four in the morning. On taking the town we were subjected to concerted counter-attacks from the Germans with one group trying to break in from the north while another tried to break out. We had practised this attack back round Rimini and it went to plan. The rest of the town was cleared and a load of Germans taken prisoner.

As the fighting began to subside we waited for an officer to kid the Germans that the rest of 8th Army had arrived and it would be an idea for them to surrender. In the end around 1,000 Germans surrendered and we kept them under lock and key in a large compound.

Overnight 'B' Company moved into Poggio Renatico to relieve 'A' Company, and one of the early morning patrols made contact with some New Zealanders who were advancing south from Reno. 'A' Company now began the advance to St Agoutino with the 17/21st Lancers and soon after they made contact with the tanks of an American Armored Division advancing south. To the elated men it seemed that enemy resistance south of the Po was virtually at an end.

Now 7RB moved to an area ten miles south of Ferrara for a rest and to prepare for the next assault across the Po River. But this rest was much shorter than expected as within two days they heard that the Guards Brigade and New Zealanders had crossed the Po almost unopposed. Ordered back to the frontline, they advanced quickly towards Adige, where they halted at Casa Odo between Adige and Padua. Here they were told that 6th Armoured Division was to go no further north. As they settled down for what they assumed would be a long stay, it seemed that for Henry and his companions the war was finally over. But fate hadn't quite finished with them yet.

Chapter 13

I Was Determined Not to Lose this Carrier: I Had Only Had it Two Weeks

Unfortunately the men's delight at being told they were to go no further was short lived. No sooner had they started to relax then they were ordered to move as fast as possible to Udine with the 27th Lancers. They passed through Padua in the dead of night and soon made contact with an American combat force which had arrived from the left flank:

> We had a blow, and then were off towards Udine and the old Great War battlefields. We reached the Piave River, crossed, and then headed for the Tagliamento River.
>
> Our next objective was Treviso near the Austrian border. Our battalion moved off and hurried towards Ferrara with the Germans trying to stop us. This is where the job of the scout platoon came in. We had to find the enemy then, instead of withdrawing, take them on and hope to fix them in position so they could be dealt with. On this occasion like many others, just three carriers edged up the road and just nine men, with the vehicles spaced so that the last carrier could escape to warn the company. The Germans usually made life difficult, mining both road and verges to slow your advance so they could prepare a hot reception when they wanted to. Sometimes we reversed up the road if there

were plenty of mines so that any blast was taken by the rear of the carrier. Each carrier carried a radio so you were always in contact with the rest of the company. We kept going until the Germans fired on us. It did play on your nerves rather.

They continued apace towards Piave but they now found that all the bridges were down so they could go no further. As it had turned into a race to see who could reach the Austrian frontier first and they were determined not to be beaten, they turned back to Treviso. Here they made their way back onto the northerly route which enabled them to sweep over the Piave and the Tagliamento River before anyone else. They now found themselves going from village to village, each time greeted with flowers, wine, and cheering, and clapping crowds. As they neared the edge of each village the church bells would ring out to notify the next village of their arrival and the process was repeated. Although the men were gratified by the tumultuous welcome, they were also wary as they knew that it was not over yet. The Germans might be withdrawing but they had not surrendered and were still not beaten. Although the greeting seemed genuine there was always the chance that there were German snipers or a few determined soldiers providing a rearguard just around the next corner. So while they enjoyed the flowers and the wine and the adulation they remained vigilant.

Just short of St Vito, near the Tagliamento, they finally caught up with the scattered remnants of the retreating German Army. Darkness was falling and no action was possible so they settled down for the night and prepared to attack at dawn the next morning. There was little sleep for the men who knew the Germans were so close and as the sun rose into the early morning sky they attacked. So successful were they that they pursued the retreating Germans past St Vito and in a short skirmish on the Tagliamento several hundred prisoners and a number of tanks were captured.

On 1 May 1945 SS General Karl Wolff and Commander-in-Chief of Army Group C, General Heinrich von Vietinghoff, ordered all German Armed Forces in Italy to cease hostilities. Despite this, on the same day, 7RB faced more opposition on the Tagliamento in the form of two tanks which they swiftly dispatched.

They were now several miles ahead of their nearest rivals and, having lost contact with Division and Brigade, they had no option but to continue to head for Udine. They met no further opposition and having arrived they used the causeway to cross the River Tagliamento into the town. Here they were met by upward of 20,000 people cheering, clapping, crying and laughing. They welcomed them with flowers and wine, hugs and kisses, their arms flung round their liberators in sheer delight. At the back of the crowds stood several armed partisans firing excited volleys into the air. The Brigade made their way slowly through the cheering crowds and eventually reached the far end of the town where they proceeded to block the north, east and south exits. But it was not quite over. By late afternoon they had reached the northern part of the town where they came across German tanks. At first it appeared as if the tanks were going to surrender but when the officer moved forward on foot to speak to the German Tank Commander he was shot by another German officer with a pistol and seriously wounded. A fierce fire fight ensued in which several riflemen were injured, one of whom later died. As darkness began to fall the anti-tank guns were brought up and managed to knock out one of the tanks. But as the night closed in the others disappeared into the darkness and by the morning there was no sign of them.

Their stay in Udine was brief as only twenty-four hours later they were ordered to head east. Their task was to prevent Chetnik and Tito forces from further fighting and to persuade Tito's men against advancing west of Goriza, a town they already held. Contact was soon made with the 20,000 Chetnik forces who quickly agreed to withdraw through the brigade to a concentration area near Palmanova. Trying to persuade Tito's men not to advance however was a good deal trickier. Unable to use force against their ally, their only option was to block the roads to delay any forward movement. This would allow the Chetniks time to withdraw as agreed. Despite several dicey moments this was successfully achieved although it was very close, with Tito's men arriving at Cormons minutes after the last of the Chetniks had left.

Having achieved their objective the 1st Guards Brigade now moved in to relieve them and they moved back towards Udine. Once in Udine they were ordered to make their way north to the Tarvisio Pass. On their way they encountered more opposition from Germany Army Group South who were still resisting as they considered they were not covered by the surrender which had just been announced. They were now flanked on either side by 2RB and 1KRRC who were also advancing to Tarvisio and who were also being held up by numerous demolitions, booby traps, mines and determined rearguard action. Moving through with them was 1KRRC with 27 L and B Sqn 1 Derby Yeo, and they finally began to make some progress against the German Army Group South.

With the end of the war in sight there was a decided sense of suppressed elation amongst the men as they pursued the Germans relentlessly towards the frontier. Having survived this far there was almost a feeling among some of them that they were safe and nothing could get them now. For others self-preservation made them considerably more cautious. Henry fell into the first category and by the time they reached the Austrian border he was almost 'bomb happy'.[1]

During the Italian campaign advances were measured in as little as a few yards. When the Germans thought you had gone far enough they stopped you. This happened again during our headlong rush towards the Austrian border. Again it was a force of tanks which held up the advance. They were hidden off the road in the tree line outside of a village. They would be hard to move so it was decided to use artillery.

The battalion halted and was nose to tail along the approach to the village. A few Shermans were with us and they refused to move until the German tanks were dealt with. Everyone knew the war was drawing to an end, so self-preservation was the order of the day. This was a job for a Bren carrier. The order was to take an officer to the next village so he could climb the church tower and call down the guns. There was only one problem: the village was occupied by the Germans and to reach it you had to go across a viaduct in full view of the German tanks.

Bombhead called the battalion forward. Standing on the side of the road he watched the Bren carriers pass, then, when I drew level told me to pull my carrier to one side. Morgan and Horace dismounted to be replaced by an officer and his servant. The officer carried a portable radio so I decided to get up a head of steam first and turned the carrier around, narrowly missing Bombhead's toes. I headed to the end of the village street, spun the carrier around, put my foot down and roared out at forty miles an hour. All the blokes gave a cheer as I speed past with the officer and his servant lying in the bottom of the carrier. Why the officer bought his servant with him I will never know, but as I left the village it must have looked like one of those fairground duck shoots to the German tank crews.

The fire from these tanks was alarming – most was solid armour piercing – but as I was quite close and travelling at such a speed they found it difficult to get a bead on me. Soon the tanks forgot about trying to knock me off the viaduct and switched to firing high explosive at the cross-roads through which I had to travel. I had very little time to work out a plan; my brain was puzzling what to do, so I decided to see if a Bren carrier could fly.

You have never lived until you have taken to the air in an armoured vehicle at 40mph and then landed 20ft below the viaduct. I shot off towards the village with the tanks still trying their luck firing at the dust as I used the viaduct as cover. All this time the officer and his servant had been trying to dig in at the bottom of the carrier. They both looked very pale but I was determined not to lose this carrier as I had only had it for two weeks.

Eventually we reached the village. As are many in Italy, the village church was on the outskirts so the officer on his shaky legs wobbled up to the top of the tower. His servant made several attempts to light a fag, and as I was by now fed up with mess tins I went off looking for a cup, saucer and plate. I found a large house and stepped smartly inside and liberated my bits of china as well as a KFS. Blimey I almost had a dinner service. So feeling dead pleased with myself I strolled back to the carrier and walked straight into a couple of Ted Paratroopers. In all the excitement I'd forgotten the village was held by the opposition. Both sides eyed each other. I was dressed like an Eyetie while the two Germans were armed to the teeth and each had a push bike. I muttered 'Buongiorno' and strolled off with my dinner set. The Teds must have had the wind up too because both jumped on their bikes and peddled off towards their lines.

The officer did bring down the artillery on to the tanks. For this he was awarded the MC (Military Cross). His servant did eventually light his fag and I got my dinner service. On arriving back at battalion to a cheer from the rest of the blokes, I was met by Bombhead who could only say 'Well done, but next time don't show off'.

Despite the German cease-fire in Italy they still couldn't afford to relax completely. Although the war was obviously lost there remained several bands of fanatical German rearguards who were still determined to prevent the Allied advance into Austria:

Most of the actions which followed were small affairs. German rearguards were off balance by the speed of our advance but even so they could still pull you up short. On one such occasion as we neared Treviso the lead platoon came under accurate mortar and small-arms fire. There was nothing for it but stop, dismount and take up a position in a nearby farm. Casualties mounted and a sergeant was hit in the stomach by bomb fragments, so me and another rifleman tried to treat the wound. I used my fingers to push his intestines back into his stomach while he kept trying to undo his belt which caused his stomach to bubble out. My hands were covered in muck and grime so if this didn't kill him nothing would. Our MO (Medical Officer) finally arrived. He had been delayed by mortar and sniper fire and was only able to look over my shoulder to see what was going on. He then rummaged about in his medical bag and produced a dressing of some sort. The MO said later my prompt action had saved the sergeant's life, but to be honest any soldier would do the same.

Every village posed a potential threat to the troops as the enemy continued to fight tenaciously for every position. For the civilians of these villages the war carried on as the Germans retreated from street to street, house to house, all the while demonstrating a total disregard for their presence:

Our battalion's advance carried on at a pace. We stopped again and dispersed in and around another small Italian town. There was now time to organize ourselves before we entered Treviso and then cross into Austria. The scout platoon found a church courtyard and parked the Bren carriers. Most of the town was either mined or demolished. German rearguards were still in the vicinity and they kept up sporadic mortar fire. The church catacombs were full of civilians, mostly women and children, but others had been caught in the blast of a mortar bomb and lay outside a nearby house. An Italian doctor arrived and said that some of the casualties were wounded and asked for help to remove these on a stretcher. The whole area was under observation and received mortar and sniper fire. None of the blokes wanted to know, especially at this stage of the war. I, however, after all my near misses, considered I must be leading a charmed life, so I volunteered. Four of us, me and three Eyeties, shuttled the wounded back to a safer place accompanied by the sound of crumps from mortars. Three of the wounded were men, two with lower-leg wounds, the third with a lump of fragment in his arse, the fourth a woman. She was six months pregnant and a shell fragment had hit her square in the stomach. Now that the wounded were recovered the doctor got to work.

141

We had a supply of carbolic soap on the carriers so the doctor was able to sterilise his hands with the water from the church fountain. He asked someone to hold down the woman who needed to be restrained while he tried to remove the fragment from her stomach. With her unborn child dead the woman lasted only a few minutes as the doctor tried to save her. I felt the life ebbing away from her before she died.

After this we moved into an abandoned house, which after looking for booby traps, we occupied for a couple of hours. The Germans continued to use sporadic mortar fire, but compared to what had gone before it was rather light. This was the last time my carrier crew was together. Our gunner Horace Kinney set off a ratchet mine under the step in the doorway which seriously damaged his leg. Everyone else had at one time or another walked across the same threshold with no problem. We heard a loud bang, which everyone thought was a mortar bomb landing, and then Horace hopped in to announce that he had stepped on a mine and his leg was hanging off inside his trousers. He collapsed and was semi-conscious. A tourniquet was applied and we carried him out on a door, still under mortar fire. We dropped him on a couple of occasions as mortar bombs landed, but we eventually got him back to the MO who was able to save Horace's life, but alas not his leg.

On 2 May all German forces in Italy were ordered to surrender unconditionally to the Allies. The war in Italy was finally over. Between September 1943 and April 1945 over 60,000 Allied and 50,000 German soldiers died in Italy. Overall, Allied casualties totalled over 320,000 with Axis casualties totalling 336,650 and this excluded those who were involved in the final surrender.

But although the war in Italy had finally reached its conclusion it was still not the end for 61st Infantry Brigade. The situation in the north was very confused. Most Germans were surrendering but others covering the approaches to the Austrian frontier through Tarvisio did not consider themselves part of the surrender. Further east large bodies of Yugoslav troops and partisans were swarming into Austrian territory, hoping to stake a claim to the land. Heavily-armed Italian partisans, both monarchists and communists, were everywhere. They were trigger happy and spoiling for a fight with whoever got in their way as well as each other.

There was also confusion as to how to treat the Germans, as orders differed depending on whether they gave themselves up before or after the surrender. Those who gave up before were treated as POWs and evacuated to Italian POW camps, whilst those who gave up after the surrender were to be labelled Surrendered Enemy Personnel and treated differently.

On VE Day 61st Infantry Brigade reached Chiusaforte and just before dawn they crossed the frontier into Austria. At 8am the German Commander surrendered the frontier to the Divisional Commander and the battalion, together with two squadrons of Lancers, led the 6th Armoured Division and 8th Army into Austria. The view from the Croce Pass was unforgettable as they gazed down on the Austrian villages that glittered in the early morning sun. As they made their way down into the valleys the countryside that greeted them was a complete contrast to the devastation that had been so commonplace in Italy. Here everything appeared clean, pristine and totally unspoilt:

> Compared with what we left behind in Italy, Austria wasn't that knocked about. Everything seemed so clean and tidy.
>
> Orders came for 61st Infantry Brigade to go full tilt for the Austrian/Yugoslav border, sweep any German resistance away and head for the area around Klagenfurt before Tito's Partisans arrived. Bombhead was in his element, nothing was to get in our way and we reached Klagenfurt half an hour before Tito's forces. Klagenfurt and the nearby lake were in the battalion area, the second battalion went to Linz.

Once across the border they were directed to go to Klagenfurt and secure all public buildings and utilities before the arrival of Tito's forces. As they sped through the countryside they were greeted by several thousand released POWs and crowds of seemingly-happy Austrians.

On 3 May 1945 General Lohr of Army Group E declared Klagenfurt an open city and on 8 May British Troops entered the city. They were met by the new democratic state authorities in front of the Stauderhaus and they immediately seized all the public buildings and utilities.

By midday battalion HQ was set up in the old Nazi Party HQ, guards were placed on all the public utilities, and all the roads coming into town were blocked. They were only just in time.

Note

1. Lawrence's words but probably quite accurate.

Chapter 14

The Battle of Dava Bridge

Three hours later groups of partisans arrived in the town on a train they had seized in the Rosenthal Valley the previous day. At the same time Yugoslav regular forces of the IV army moved in. Both laid claim to the city and its surrounding area and set about trying to establish a Carinthian Military Zone. They forced their way through the streets which were packed with refugees and soldiers of various nationalities until they reached Neuer Platz where they came face to face with British Armoured vehicles:

> Our battalion occupied all vulnerable points as the partisans began infiltrating into the town. To make sure there was no chance of fire being exchanged with our 'allies' we were ordered to stand guard with only pick helves.

The intention of Tito's forces was to set up a government in Klagenfurt which was the capital of Carinthia, an area which they claimed was theirs. After some tense negotiations they were allowed in and the town was jointly occupied by both British and Tito's men which was a very complicated situation and fraught with difficulty.

On 7 May, knowing that Tito's forces were heading towards the city, the provisional government asked the residents to decorate their homes with the Carinthian colours. Having freed themselves from association with the Nazis they were also now flying the Austrian flag outside City Hall. The first point of contention came when the Yugoslav military immediately demanded the removal of the Austrian flag which was flying from the City Hall and ordered

145

them to fly the Yugoslav flag. Captain Watson immediately pro-
hibited this but also ordered that the Austrian flag be taken down.
Furious that their flag was not flying, a Yugoslav emissary, accompanied by an armed partisan, entered the building and demanded
that the acting State Governor repeal the order to remove it. This
was ignored.

The situation remained fraught for several days while the British
sought to keep the peace until a diplomatic solution could be found.
For Henry life was just as busy as before but a lot more complicated.
Firstly there was some confusion as to whether the Austrians should
be treated as victims of Nazi occupation or as the enemy. The city
was also full of thousands of refugees any of whom might be one
of Tito's partisans. They all had to be policed and watched as did
the city's indigenous population. Although most were friendly and
delighted that the British were there, others were not so friendly. So,
not only did they have increased guard duties, they also had to be
diplomatic when dealing with those threatening them; something
they found rather difficult having spent the last two years fighting
for their lives:

> Taking advantage of the situation, the partisans began
> abducting Austrian women and children back into
> Yugoslavia. We put a stop to this with force, armed
> to the teeth and supported by tanks. The partisans soon got
> the message when faced by veteran troops.

The main task of the occupying force was to round up the
remnants of the German army and disarm them and to deal with
the thousands of refugees who were continuing to arrive from every
direction:

> At about the same time Tito's forces arrived, the remains of
> German Army Group South came into surrender to local
> British forces. The Germans and their allies were hindered
> by Tito's partisans and one hell of a battle broke out near
> the border with Austria.

The occupation was only three days old when they received news that the German Balkan Army group was advancing on Klagenfurt from Yugoslavia to surrender. The German Balkan Army was about a hundred thousand strong and had members of several different nationalities. Without recourse to the British, Tito's forces decided that they would accept the surrender instead and carry out the disarming themselves. They set up a roadblock on the Dava Bridge some five miles south of the British roadblock, which was on the southern outskirts of Klagenfurt, and waited for the Germans to arrive. As they did, fierce arguments broke out. Before long these developed into a fire fight and then the Germans and Tito's forces became locked in deadly combat. By dawn the following day news reached the British that Tito's forces were in trouble. The Germans had taken the bridge and Tito's forces had fled to the hills leaving the only two tanks they had burning by the side of the road. It now took the British several hours of negotiations to persuade the German commanders to surrender. Eventually they succeeded and for the next four days 7RB stood guard as the German Balkan Army trekked wearily from Yugoslavia to Austria and into camps:

> I was on duty with an officer to supervise the surrender of German forces which included Russians, Ukrainians, and several other nationalities. They filed past in a never ending column. They'd had enough but still conducted themselves in a soldiery manner as they laid down their arms.
>
> The prisoners were kept in fields. Being there reminded me of the pre-war country fairs; everywhere you looked there were tents. Having no intention of surrendering to the Russians the soldiers had also brought their families to surrender. There were horses and wagons to add to this throng. Among the surrendered were several thousand SS. Their officers still had fight left in them and they spat at us when they handed over their weapons. One or two received a smack in the ear for their trouble.
>
> Bombhead, now promoted Lieutenant Colonel, had the pick of the horses (his brother Fred Darling was a famous

racehorse trainer). He selected a huge 18-hands monster nicknamed 'King Kong' after the film monster. He also picked a nice Mercedes staff car to go with his turretless Stuart recce tank. A bridge in Italy was also christened 'Bombhead Bridge' where he used a Sherman to pull the battalion's lead carrier platoon across the river as bridge was damaged. The engineers later constructed a Bailey Bridge which was later christened with his name.

The battle of the Dava Bridge that took place between the Germans and Tito's forces was more or less the last shots of the war. Within days Tito's forces had withdrawn back across the border and things began to relax slightly:

> Once Tito's men withdrew back into Yugoslavia we finally began to relax although all the time we kept an eye on Tito's partisans on the border. The battalion now arranged a series of parades for the locals. There was friendly competition with the Guards as to who could put on the best turnout and marching drill. The battalion band entertained the Austrians with military marches and a few more familiar tunes. Horse races were arranged and leave granted to go to the Worthersee Lake.

With Tito's troops back across the border and the arrival of more replacement troops, things began to relax. Guard duties decreased so they were able to take part in other activities. A battalion stable was built up from the numerous captured horses. A mounted troop of Riflemen was formed and regular race meetings, gymkhanas and horse shows were held. The 6th Armoured Division ran at least one race meeting a fortnight. Football was also organized and a combined 2RB and 7RB team won the 6th Armoured Divisional Knockout Competition against the Guards Brigade in the Sports Platz in Klagenfurt. There was also the opportunity for boating, fishing, swimming, cricket, athletics, mountaineering and other sports. Theatre and cinemas were also popular and for Henry and the battle weary men it finally started to feel as if the war was really over.

The British had confiscated all Nazi property and frozen all bank accounts and financial transactions when they first arrived. The challenge now was to get these and basic communication channels working as quickly as possible. However it was to take several months before the postal service, supply routes and public transport were working again properly.

But for Henry it was a time to relax. For the first time in two years he forgot to worry about whether he would survive and instead he started to look forward to the day when he could finally go home. He joined in the activities and spent his time exploring his surroundings. One building in particular drew his attention:

There was this camp where all the top-ranking German officers went. All sorts – army, navy, fighter aces and U-boat captains. It seems that they went there to consort with women who were to have children by these blokes for the Fuhrer. They lived off the fat of the land, but now the war was over. The youngsters had been abandoned and left to their own devices. We caught one going through the dustbins, adopted him and fitted him out with a battledress.

The German POWs carried on doing fatigues up in Austria. Most were paratroopers and they were kept in one of the castles which dotted the countryside. These were the same men we had fought in the Arno Valley and on the approaches to Florence. On one occasion I and a couple of my mates received an invitation to dinner from the family who owned the schloss (castle) so in our best BD we strolled up for a convivial evening away from the battalion lines. What a surprise awaited us, for about a dozen German paratroopers had also received the same invitation. There was a strict code of non-fraternisation enforced, but this seemed not to be the case here. Both riflemen and paras eyed one another up, then the Germans shuffled along to make room on the benches for their host's new guests.

The Germans seemed a lot older than us. All were veterans of some of the bloodiest actions of the war and wore the cuff bands with Crete, Cassino etc. They knew our reputation from the battles we fought against them in Italy, but we riflemen looked so young up against these blokes. These paratroopers were some of the finest soldiers in the world and now they did fatigues for us riflemen.

Henry was still thoroughly enjoying himself in Austria. Taking part in all the sporting activities gave him the opportunity to try and forget some of the horrific things he had seen and the traumatic events he had witnessed. But there was a bitter-sweet side to his relaxation. Being free to play football and to take part in athletics competitions without people trying to kill him reminded him of his life before he had been conscripted and he began to long for the time when he could go home.

In August they moved to a new area near Kuhnsdorf and Eisenkeppel and began settling down for the winter. There was still no news of when they would be de-mobbed and Henry resigned himself to another Christmas away from those he loved. At this rate his girlfriend would find someone else, especially now the war was over and so many men were back in England. Still there were worse places to be and with a bit of luck this would be the last year away. And he consoled himself that he was at least with his mates. But things were about to change yet again.

Not long after they arrived in their new rest area a telegram arrived from GHQ in Naples with the codeword 'Minerva' on. This signified orders to be ready to move to Egypt at seven days' notice. The battalion was immediately reorganized and anyone who had been overseas for longer than two years was told they were not eligible for further service in the Far East. The old hands were delighted. They had finally won the right to go home. But not Henry. He had missed out by a matter of weeks. Instead he dejectedly packed up his kit and prepared for the long, tedious journey back to North Africa. The battalion left Austria on 20 August 1945 and began the journey to Port Said:

Our stay in Austria did not last very long. Civil unrest broke out in Egypt so our battalion and the Black Watch

150

entrained once more for the Middle-East. The older rifle-men were hoping that they would leave the battalion in Austria and head for home which many of them did. Many young soldiers now joined the ranks and the battalion was different from the one that ended the war in Austria.

Our battalion underwent a long train journey from Austria, through Italy to Naples. The ship we were to take back to the Middle-East was full of New Zealanders on their way home. They had completed their three years overseas service and were delighted at having a go at us as we had to soldier on. By now our battalion had a band and to make the crossing easier they gave a concert on the lower deck. An officer then appeared from another regiment and requisitioned the band for a dance with the servicewomen also on the boat. Needless to say we were not happy when we did not receive an invitation.

To the cheers of the New Zealanders, our blokes stormed the upper deck scattering all and sundry, and our officers did not interfere, but stood to one side sipping their whiskey and sodas while taking note of the ring leaders. The ship's RSM tried to restore order by standing on a chair and attempting to read the riot act but he was sent flying and broke his leg. Another ship's officer was threatened with being thrown over the side, and some of the blokes stormed the engine room and stopped the ship. We now had a mutiny on our hands.

Any of those veteran infantry battalion, men who had spent three years fighting Germans, would have reacted the same. Certainly a few KARs were not going to bother them.

Chapter 15

Port Said, 1 September: The Last Post

There was silence on the quay as the officer in charge considered how best to deal with the crisis unfolding in front of him. These were not green troops but seasoned veterans. Furthermore they were veteran Riflemen and they were needed to do a job in Egypt. Yes, he could try and order the KARs to overpower them but he was unlikely to be successful. More likely he would have a bloodbath on his hands and if that happened he could kiss goodbye to his career, let alone any promotion. He considered talking to them but they did not seem in any mood to listen and the longer he stood there the more angry they seemed to become.

The stalemate continued. The men were motionless in the heat of the day, and the only signs of stress were the small beads of sweat glistening on the tanned skin above their lips. He looked at the KARs. They too were motionless but he felt uneasy as he realised that if he ordered them to open fire on their comrades-in-arms they might refuse and he would have yet another mutiny on his hands.

It was an extremely hot day. The sun was now beating down uninterrupted from a cloudless blue sky and he could feel the beads of sweat on his forehead running down his nose and into his mouth. He licked his lips nervously; the droplets tasted sour and salty, the taste of fear. He could feel the sweat begin to cool on his back making him shiver and he realised that he would have to do something and do it soon.

'Get Bombhead to come and sort this out.' He had no idea where the voice came from even though he scoured their faces looking for clues. But there was nothing. The men stared back sullenly. There was no movement; all the sounds of the quayside seemed to have receded into the distance as the stalemate continued. He would have like nothing better than to have complied, to have handed over the whole mess to someone else, but unfortunately Bombhead, their affectionate name for their Commanding Officer, was not available.

Henry was as motionless as the others and the longer he stood there the more angry he became. He had been fighting for over two years and wanted nothing more than to go home, but he had followed orders without complaint – well, with lots of chuntering and grumbling perhaps, but he had still obeyed. This mess was not of their making. It had been caused by the insensitive behaviour of an officer from another battalion who had seen fit to ride roughshod over them. The whole mess could have been averted if their own officers had intervened when the first officer tried to appropriate their band but they hadn't. They had sat back and let things take their course. He could feel his anger rising and he took a deep breath in an attempt to calm down. The last thing he wanted was to spend the next seven years in the 'glasshouse' but at the same time he was not prepared to back down.

It seemed as if they had all been standing there for hours even though it was nothing like that long. The tension, if anything, had risen and Henry began to wonder if they would ever get out of this. The officer stood there indecisively for several more moments before suddenly speaking: 'Right men I think this has gone far enough.' His voice started off slightly nervously but as he warmed to his theme his voice became more authoritative. 'It's very hot standing here. We've all had a long journey and I think it's time we moved off to somewhere a little cooler. What do you say we forget this ever happened – and the incident on the ship of course,' he added hastily as a voice in the crowd started to speak. 'We just walk away from here and the British Army forgets? Yeah right!' This time the voice was incredulous and the men began muttering amongst themselves.

154

'Look we can't ask Colonel Darling to sort this out because he isn't here as you well know. He left in July. Why don't you all just lower your weapons and then we can get on with the job we've come here to do?'

He was greeted with silence and then one of the men near the front spat on the ground. There was a low murmuring among the men and then silence. The officer looked round hoping for something more conciliatory but they returned his gaze sullenly. Realising he was getting nowhere, he hesitated for another few moments and then turned round and went back up the gangplank to the ship leaving the two opposing units of Riflemen facing each other with weapons drawn. Now the officer had gone the tension lessened imperceptibly and Henry glanced at the man next to him. 'So what do you think?' he asked quietly. The man shrugged. 'Don't know, but we're not in the wrong so we're going to stand firm.' The last part was said defiantly and despite the seriousness of the situation Henry found himself smiling. 'Too right,' the man behind him answered before he had time to speak.

'Not really gonna fire on your fellow riflemen are you?' The question came from someone further back and was aimed at the Corporal of the KARs. The eyes of everyone there were now focused on the Corporal who swallowed nervously but didn't answer. 'Course they wouldn't. They're Riflemen like us aren't they?' The question provoked some laughter which eased the tension slightly but neither side lowered their rifles.

The silence lengthened, the sun rose higher in the sky and the heat became oppressive. There was little breeze coming off the sea and the air was still. The men remained motionless and the clock ticked on. Eventually they heard the unmistakable sound of a staff car speeding towards them. It slid to an abrupt halt and Lieutenant Colonel Vivian Street climbed out. They recognised him immediately as he had been 2i/c under Douglas Darling (Bombhead) for most of the Italian Campaign and they knew he had taken over when Bombhead left in July 1945. He was a pre-war London Rifle Brigade man who had later been seconded to the SAS and they knew they could trust him. Henry could never really remember what had been said, only that within minutes they were lowering their rifles and their 'mutiny' was over.

The official records show that although the battalion arrived on 1 September they did not officially disembark until 2 September. They were then sent by train to Moascar and lodged temporarily in 153 transit camp. After two weeks in the transit camp they moved to slightly more comfortable quarters in the permanent barrack buildings in Moascar Garrison:

> The battalion was sent to a camp on the Suez Canal (Moascar) then two companies were sent to Mena for guard duties in Cairo. Our battalion stayed in Cairo for several months guarding vulnerable points and other British interests while the army let things cool down. Our stay there was seen by most of us as punishment for our mutiny, but the army would not admit this.[1]

It was quite unusual that the army did not pursue the matter with any vigour as they did not normally allow men to mutiny without some kind of punishment. But at the time they had other more serious problems to deal with which may go some way to explaining this.

At the beginning of April 1945 when it was obvious that the war would soon be finishing, plans began to be made to return troops to their countries of origin. The 6th South African Armoured Division, together with various other South Africans who had been serving in other divisions and corps, would need transportation back to South Africa for demobilisation. By 1 May it was realised that no plans had yet been made so the Union Defence Force began making preparations. The South African Air Force's 1 and 5 Wings were merged into 4 Group to be used as a shuttle service to move 5,000 troops per month beginning on 1 July. A further 15,000 men were transported by sea during the second half of the year. This should mean that around 45,000 men would be repatriated by the end of 1945. However, in addition to the troops mentioned there were also other troops in Italy plus thousands of troops from the 2nd South

African Infantry who were captured at Sidi Rezegh and Tobruk and who had recently been released from POW camps in Italy. These men had not been included in the demobilization plans.

The staging depot was at Helwan north of Cairo and was soon very overcrowded. Designed to hold 5,000 men it was soon holding upwards of 9,000. Although it was announced on 9 August that ships would be arriving to transport 3,000 to 5,000 men back home, less than a week later they were told the shipping would be delayed. Food was now in short supply and there were not enough chefs which meant queues for what food there was were long. Trading rights to anything other than the NAFFI were controlled by Egyptians and the men felt they were being exploited by inflated prices. Even the two cinemas, which were meant to alleviate some of the tension, caused problems as men bought tickets only to find there was not enough space to get in.

Things deteriorated even further as the new arrivals were split up alphabetically by surname and then again by their demobilization category which in turn was based on when they had been sent overseas. This meant unit structures disappeared and men were grouped with soldiers and NCOs they did not know. To add insult to injury 500 volunteers were then called for, irrespective of their demob category, to go home as a priority and assist in the demobilization process back in South Africa.

On 20 August a meeting was held and over 1,500 men attended. As more arrived the meeting became heated and violence erupted. The soldiers then rioted, smashing, looting and trashing everything in sight beginning with the two Egyptian-owned cinemas which they set on fire. They then split up and set fire to other Egyptian premises included book stalls, cars, houses, bungalows, one of their own messes and also looted the NAAFI store.

General Poole from 6th Armoured Division flew in from Italy to calm things down and promised that the rate of repatriation would be speeded up. The housing of troops was immediately carried out on a unit basis to restore discipline and a brigadier was appointed to command the depot. A public address system was installed so that troops could be kept up to date with the news, and free outdoor film shows were set up. On 26 August the DGQ-A of Italy and Egypt

157

appointed a court of enquiry which reported that overcrowding, continual delays and the failure to airlift the promised number of troops had been contributing factors. Whereas initial announcements had said 500 a day would be repatriated, the average figure during the whole of July had only been 108. The damage from the rioting caused was assessed as costing upward of £22,768,431. But as far as the South Africans were concerned things now speeded up and by 25 January 1946, 101,676 men had been repatriated and the last flight took place on 26 January.

But this was just one of the problems facing the British. The reasons given for sending Henry and the rest of the battalion to Egypt had been because of an upsurge in the nationalist movement that wanted all the British out of Egypt. There had also been a rise in anti-Jewish feelings, aggravated by the number of refugees arriving from Europe.

There had been a British military presence in Egypt since 1882 and the country had been declared a British protectorate in 1914. The Egyptians had been granted limited independence in 1922 and negotiations for the withdrawal of the British military presence began. The negotiations had dragged on interminably and there was continual unrest as the Egyptians resented the continued British presence.

In 1936 a treaty of alliance was finally signed allowing the British to maintain a continued presence in the Suez Canal Zone but to gradually withdraw its military presence from elsewhere in Egypt. This had still not taken place by the time the Second World War started and the now considerably enhanced British military presence provoked even more discontent. Negotiations continued throughout the war but the apparent lack of progress finally provoked a spate of anti-British violence in both Alexandria and Cairo in 1945 and 1946. The Egyptian authorities struggled to prevent attacks on British property and personnel but although British units and reinforcements were sent to both cities they were not actually used to restore order, only to protect British property and personnel.

By the end of September the battalion was given the task of providing guards for VIPs in the Cairo District. Twenty-four-hour guards had now been put on HBM Embassy and the residences of

'C' in 'C' Middle East and GOC BTE. 'A' and 'B' Companies were formed into a detachment under Odgers and given a large numbers of less-important guards and police duties to carry out. On 1 October they moved to Mena which Henry remembered from the days of the conference back in 1943. Their official guard duty began on 4 October.

To start with things were reasonably quiet but the air of discontent and threat of unrest was never far from the surface. There had been a rise in anti-Semitism in Egyptian nationalist and intellectual circles since the 1930s, mainly in response to the Arab struggle in Palestine, pro-Nazi sympathies and the rise of Egyptian nationalism and religious fundamentalism. However the position of Jewish communities in Egypt had been relatively stable until the second half of 1945. As October drew to a close there was a call for mass demonstrations against Zionism on 2 November (the 28th Anniversary of the Balfour Declaration) in all major Egyptian cities by Egyptian nationalists and Islamist groups such as Misr-al-Fatat, the Muslim Brotherhood and the Young Men's Muslim Association. A report by the British Commissioner of Cairo written three days before the demonstrations noted 'considerable ill feeling against Jews ...' but that '... security measures were in place.'

On Friday 2 November the violence that had been simmering under the surface finally erupted and anti-Jewish and anti-British demonstrations began. Ten Jewish people were killed and 350 injured as several Jewish buildings were burned down or damaged. These included the Ashkenazi synagogue where sacred texts, some over 1,000 years old, were thrown on bonfires. The Jewish soup kitchen, shelter for homeless Jewish people, Jewish hospital, old people's home and the Arts Society quarters as well as several other Jewish-owned businesses were attacked while mobs of students roamed the streets shouting 'Death to the Jews'. The disturbances did not stop with the Jewish quarter and soon spread to Coptic, Greek Orthodox and Catholic institutions. In all, over 500 businesses were looted and one policeman killed. The police lost control at one point and had to send for reinforcements. Cairo was placed out of bounds for all Allied troops and British armoured cars with armoured Egyptian troops, and mounted Egyptian police patrolled the streets on the Friday night enforcing the 8pm curfew.

By 4 November there had been over 900 arrests, half the shops remained closed and the police were patrolling the streets in force. British army trucks rode through the streets collecting British and other Allied troops and removing them from the area as Cairo was placed out of bounds for the second successive day. Mobs paraded through the streets looting and destroying anything in their path, throwing stones and whatever else was to hand. Over 300 people were injured by gunshot wounds as the police in steel helmets opened fire in an attempt to disperse the daytime mobs which in some cases were estimated to be up to 60,000 strong. Eventually the police gained control and things gradually quietened down:

> In December we moved from Moascar to Tahag, from a hot camp with few amenities to a dustier one without even a NAAFI, while a detachment for guard duties moved from the dust devils of Mena to a barracks at Abbassia.

The rioting that had begun in November reached its peak in February with attacks on British service clubs and other service property. On 21 February the Communist-led National Committee of Workers and Students called a strike, completely shutting down the country. The Barracks at Kasr el Nil which housed the District HQ came under heavy siege after the crowd tried to stop three British lorries entering the barracks. The first driver reversed and was able to escape but the second was stopped and dragged out by the crowd. The crowd began throwing missiles at the barracks and then lighted torches. Because the roof was wooden there was a danger of it catching fire so British troops opened fire with machine guns. The two lorries abandoned in front of the barracks now caught fire and the crowd began to attack any car that came into the Square. It tried to force their way into the barracks but was held back by the troops who had closed the gates. The ammunition on the lorries then caught fire and began to explode, adding to the general noise and confusion but did at least drive back the crowd. An Egyptian ambulance arrived but was beaten back by the crowd and an American staff car was attacked and its driver chased by the angry crowd. The Egyptian police finally arrived and, taking advantage of a brief lull, a British officer drove up, climbed the gates and disappeared inside. The police began to put a protective cordon around the barracks as armoured cars began arriving with more troops.

As afternoon arrived the crowd began to disperse. Unable to break through the cordon protecting the barracks they now headed for Abdin Palace Square where they chanted 'Evacuation of British troops or bloodshed', 'Down with England', and 'Down with the conqueror' as two Egyptian tanks, twenty armoured cars and six lorries full of troops watched. Further clashes took place between the British and the demonstrators at Bab-el-Hadid barracks, the HQ of the Military Police who fired back wounding several. The RAF Administration building was also attacked and here people were killed when the RAF opened fire. Crowds also set fire to the RCAF HQ and the New Zealand Troops Club in the centre of the city. The South African Air HQ was also attacked and the guards there fired into the air.

Other rioters attempted to set fire to the Lady Tedder Club but were driven off while army hostels Cecil House, the Victory Club and Connaught House were burnt down. The rioters used the furniture and belongings from inside as missiles to pelt the Fire Brigade who did eventually succeed in putting the fires out. For the next few days British Embassy staff and workers at other British organisations had to be taken to work in special buses and lorries earlier than normal and then collected when it was convenient to do so.

Henry had regained his stripes while in Italy and was now a full corporal. As the riots continued he was given the task of commanding the guard on one of the main banks in Cairo. In front of the bank there were large metal gates which were closed and padlocked. Henry ordered the Bren guns to be placed at intervals along the length of the gates and they waited. In the distance they could hear the muted sounds of the crowd chanting. The sound grew louder and louder and within minutes they could see what appeared to be thousands of people coming towards them. It was obvious he did not have enough guns so Henry immediately requested more Bren guns to ensure they could hold the bank perimeter against the obvious threat of looting from the approaching rioters. By now the noise was deafening as they surged forward throwing themselves against the gates. The massive padlocks buckled with the weight of the crowd but held fast. Unable to break through, the rioters now began trying to climb the gates leaving Henry with no choice. He ordered the riflemen to open fire. The noise of the Brens firing was lost in the roar of the crowd but the bullets, as they ricocheted off the gates into the crowd, had the desired effect and before long the rioters had dispersed.

It was not just the British in Cairo that came under attack. In Alexandria where the British naval base was, demonstrators tore down British flags and stoned shops and Alexandria was also placed out of bounds for British troops. In all seventeen people were killed and 300 injured during the anti British riots in Cairo and Alexandria. Troops had to fire on rioters to protect lives of British personnel and although no British were killed there were a number of casualties. Rioters had also attempted to set fire to All Saints Cathedral leaving the floor littered with knives and other objects. The doors were broken, windows smashed and chairs smashed for firewood. The Bishop's house was also ransacked and crockery broken. During the afternoon one mob set fire to a service canteen and another attacked and burnt down a block of flats after it was claimed an Italian woman worker fired a revolver at the crowds.

In response the authorities confiscated the Wafdist newspaper *Albalagh* on the grounds it was inciting people to riot. But the worst was yet to come. At Alexandria on 4 March two military policemen manning a control point were overcome by the mob and killed. The severed head of one was displayed in triumph:

> The troubles escalated in Cairo after a couple of red caps were found castrated in a fig orchard. The battalion was needed right away and patrols in 15-cwts patrolled the street with orders to shoot anyone standing above head height and anyone who tried to jump on the back of the

lorry. Needless to say these orders were carried out on several occasions.

By April the battalion was short of men and it was obvious that to ensure they could carry out all their commitments they would have to reorganize. In addition to Cairo they were having to provide a fifty-strong detachment to guard the ships at Port Said and they were still providing men for Moascar and Tel el Kebir garrisons for police duty. But before they could be reinforced they were told the battalion was being disbanded. For Henry it could not come soon enough but after so many disappointments he was almost scared to believe that it was actually true. But on 28 April they handed over all their commitments to the 5th Battalion, The East Yorkshire Regiment, and by 29 April the whole battalion was sent to GBD at Almaza. Henry began to breathe a sigh of relief. After so much fighting, so much death and destruction it looked like it was finally time to go home. Rioting, demonstrations and strikes continued until the British evacuation to the Suez Canal Zone in the spring of 1947. During this period of unrest the British suffered eighty-four military casualties:

> The battalion was disbanded in Egypt on 14 May 1946. I returned home in June 1946, my army service since December 1941 drawing to an end. The Britain I returned to had changed in many ways, but still there was no room on a bus if you carried all your kit and everyone tuned their nose up at the sight of a squaddie. My short stay back at the Peninsula Barracks entailed whitening coal and being chased around by eighteen year-olds with one stripe. I had regained my two stripes after losing them in the desert for striking another man for pinching water. When I returned to Winchester along with all the old soldiers we were reduced to the ranks on the eve of leaving the army.
>
> The army then came along and offered me the post of Sergeant Instructor at Tidworth on Bren carriers which was ironic as I'd had so many shot from under me in the war.

I refused the posting and came out the army on 'Z' class release to start my own business.

Henry was de-mobbed on 'Z' Class release in June 1946 at the Sir John Moore Barracks, and then placed on the reserve.

Note

1. Henry was always convinced that Bombhead had something to do with the battalion being let off lightly, being an old mate of FM Sir Henry (Jumbo) Wilson, for a long time C in C in the Middle East.

Epilogue
By Lawrence Taylor

Before Dad went overseas he was engaged to a girl to whom he wrote letters home throughout his time abroad. Things went smoothly until one letter informed him that she had met someone else and got married. Dad was somewhat taken aback, but replied and told her to keep the engagement ring as a wedding present. On his return home on leave, Dad saw his former fiancée with her husband, an ex POW, who it seems offered her a proposal of marriage and a fur coat. About this time he also received a request for back taxes from the Inland Revenue:

> I had not paid tax since I joined the army, I thought it was a bloody cheek to ask me to pay, so I wrote *Bollocks* across the note and sent it back. I did not hear anything else.

On the same leave, Dad's mate George appeared on the door step one morning. He was at loggerheads with his family and did not want to go home. Dad's parents offered him a bed and this is when he met Dad's eldest sister Rose.

Dad mentioned how much the people and the country had changed. On one leave he came home with his kit, jumped on a bus and was told flatly by the woman conductor that he could not bring his kit on the bus and to get off at once. So much for a land fit for heroes. But luckily an elderly woman on the bus came to his rescue and told the conductor to stop 'Acting like Hitler' and to let the soldier on the bus. Soon the rest of the passengers chipped in, and Dad got his bus ride – but had to stand all the way by the stairs.

It was on leave that Dad met my mum. They had known one another before he went in the army. She was still at school, but both families knew one another and had frequented the same working men's club. Mum left school and went straight into war work and soon became a factory union representative in 1942 at the age of seventeen. The factory spent the war making fittings for drop tanks used by USAAF and RAF long-range fighters. The two met again after the war at the working men's club they went to before the war. Mum was there with her parents. Dad was drunk under the club's snooker table after a session with a couple of his cousins.

Employment for recently de-mobbed soldiers was scarce. Dad was a bricklayer and so went back into the building trade on peace work. This was the time of 'New Jerusalem', the new Labour government's promise to build thousands of houses and set up the welfare state. Indeed, the building trade had plenty of work and building firms which had made their name during the war cornered all the work. Bricklayers were taken on under strict union conditions. The amount of bricks to be laid in a day was restricted with the threat of dismissal if the rules were broken. Dad fell foul of these rules on a couple of occasions and like many ex soldiers decided to go it alone.

In 1946 money was short. Dad only had his de-mob suit and uniform to stand up in as his mum had cleared all his clothes out and left him with nothing on his return after the war. His mum, my grandmother, had lost a boyfriend in the First World War and did not think Dad would return. Dad cobbled together some money, bought a trowel and lines, and made a builder's level from a scaffold board. He started building front and garden walls to replace the railings removed during the war. Work was good but finding materials was difficult as Britain was still on rationing.

Dad attended two Alamein re-unions in London (1947/1948). Here he met a couple of his mates from the sniper section in Italy. Both were wounded in the cold winter months of 1944/45. One had been shot through the backside as he tried to move position, a thing you were told never to do. The other received a wound in the arm when a bullet from a German sniper entered his hand at the little finger and exited at his elbow. Dad was the only rifleman from the seven-man section to survive the war; the others were either killed or wounded. On both occasions Field Marshal Montgomery was the guest of honour, and no, he did not mention their meeting in North Africa.

By 1947 things were going from bad to worse in Britain. There was no end in sight of rationing so the black market thrived and ex-soldiers used their war time training to benefit. One of Dad's mates at the time was a former REME Major, an old desert hand who was in tank recovery. He and Dad made trips to one of the American bases in Cambridge on the Major's motor bike and sidecar. They would meet a USAF sergeant who passed over a whole pig, dead of course, for a few pounds. Then, with Dad riding behind the Major and the dead pig ensconced in the side car suitably disguised as a passenger, they roared back to Enfield. Here the pig was cut up in my grandparents' kitchen and distributed to clients around Enfield and Edmonton under cover of darkness:

> It was dodgy because the Law (police) was on the lookout. You had to watch who you spoke to in the pubs because of copper's narks (informers), so we scotched this after a few trips, besides it was the winter of 1947 and everything froze solid.

The money Dad earned helped him to move into the production of concrete blocks. His experience as a youngster in the brick fields came in handy. The making of moulds for the blocks was not a problem and his own father let him use a couple of sties on his pig farm to make and store the blocks. The heat from the pigs aided the drying process and stopped the blocks perishing in the winter frosts. My grandfather's other job was in the local Brimsdown power station in East Enfield. His experience as a RN stoker in the First World War helped him to secure the job. So it was my grandfather who created the excess ash from the boilers which went into the concrete blocks.

Business was brisk, so Dad used land adjacent to his father's piggery and started making the blocks using machines from Germany. Times were getting better and those with a trade were in demand as the Labour government carried out its promise to build a land fit for heroes. New towns began to spring up around the countryside; housing estates multiplied and new houses required building materials. As the fifties approached, Dad had branched out into edging for the new roads which serviced the boom in building and he needed some transport:

> Old army lorries were going for a song; you could buy a couple of three-tonners and they would throw in the contents in the back. The drivers were blokes who had learnt to drive in the war.

Then only one year into the new decade, the Korean War broke out and Dad was called up. To all intent and purposes Dad had pushed his time in the army to the back of his mind. His mates had long gone their own way, and but for his brother-in-law, his time in the army was forgotten. It was some time before he claimed his service and campaign medals. Then in February 1951 he received orders from the Infantry record office in Exeter to report to the HQ of 168th Lorried Infantry Brigade for training from 21 June to 4 August 1951. Before this he would have to report for a medical. With his business now growing, Dad asked for extenuating circumstances. His friend, the Major from the REME, wrote a note to support Dad's request and the call up was cancelled:

> The army had had five-and-half years of my life, busted me down to the ranks when I was de-mobbed, then they wanted me back for Korea.

Dad now had a clear run to build up his business. It was hard graft working up to sixty hours a week. Mum and Dad married in 1947. She can remember his weight dropping down to near nine stone in these days. She said: 'I can remember him coming in the Boundary (pub) after work. It had been raining hard and everywhere he stood was a pool of cement-coloured water which had run from his work clothes.'

Dad was from the generation where hard work was the order of the day. Thus, by the end of the fifties he had his own business, Alma Precast Concrete Company, and a construction firm building factories in and around Enfield. It was time to start a family.

Mum had several miscarriages before I was born in May 1959. Dad had started to build his own factory at the time and finished the build in 1961. But the human body can only take so much and in 1964 he had a serious heart attack, – then a second the day after. Doctors gave him only another fifteen years to live, but Dad being Dad was back working six months later.

With the factory leased, he looked for other things to occupy himself. He built a chicken farm to supply local shops with fresh eggs, and then started what he considered to be one of his favourite jobs, the restoration of Tudor and Elizabethan houses. I don't think he intended this at first, but a friend of his asked him to restore an Elizabethan farm house at Barwick Ford, Hertfordshire, and Dad had a crack at it. He loved it. Recommendations followed and he spent the next twelve years restoring a variety of buildings from the Tudor and Elizabethan period. I helped him during my school holidays and it was truly amazing the work he carried out.

Dad retired at the age of sixty, but being the man he was, he looked around for something to take up his time. He still did the odd building jobs but now he undertook another one of his favourite pastimes as an athletics coach. He had always enjoyed running at school and was a regular at the athletic meetings at White City in the 1940's. Now he decided to coach me. Dad soon had an athletic squad to be reckoned with at the Borough of Enfield Harriers. Most were youngsters who he coached. He wanted them to have the best chance to succeed in the sport, something he felt he lost when he went into the army. One athlete he helped coach at this time eventually competed for Great Britain in the Olympics and World Championships. I met my wife Pat during this time and we were married in 1987.

As the years of hard work and injuries sustained during the war started to catch up with him, Dad had three ulcers burst in 1986. He was very ill indeed but as usual he pulled through and carried on with his coaching. He finally called it a day in 1992 and soon after began to talk to me about his experiences in the war. We decided to write these down as he now was starting to relive some of his experiences in the form of flashbacks and nightmares. It is funny, but through his endless stories I felt in the end that I actually knew all his mates and would have liked to have met them. Some of Dad's recollections were used in another publication, (David Lee's *Up Close and Personal*), but these were but small escapades.

Dad always liked to keep himself occupied and he carried on coaching me in athletics, something I still do to this day.

My interest in military history, and the Rifle Brigade in particular, led me to join a living history group (The Rifles Living History Society). Dad's latter years were spent attending living history events where his experiences were keenly listened to. Mum died suddenly in January 2008, and Dad threw himself even more into remembering those of his generation. He became an honorary member of another living history group (Battle 4 Europe) and honorary president of The Rifles. He collected for the Royal British Legion Poppy Appeal and supported appeals for Ghurkhas and 3Rifles.

As a family we had always spent our summer holidays in Italy. During the early seventies we visited Monte Cassino and Dad took us back to visit the family in Sambuca where he had eaten the mushrooms. They of course asked him if the other soldiers had survived. Alas too many had not.

As Dad reached his mid-eighties we decided to take him back for a last time to Monte Cassino, Monte Malbe, Borgo Tossingnano and Poggio Renatico. For the first part of our holiday each year we took him back to the places which now, through our endless reminiscences, I felt I knew as well as he did. These occasions were special. He remembered every feature, every bend, and even where people had died. Visiting the Commonwealth cemeteries were always emotional experiences. Dad would stand in front to the graves of his mates and remember them as they were.

Dad's health deteriorated after our last trip to Italy in 2009 and we were unable to take him back although he always said he was up to the task. He still kept up his appearances at a few living history events, and collected for the RBL poppy appeal, but alas in the end he did what all old soldiers do, he just faded away on 22 December 2011.

Index